Praise from Teache...
Smart Fron...

Finally, a book about learning that is easy to read, fun and engaging. If children are to be successful in school they must be ready to learn. As parents that is our responsibility. **Smart From the Start** takes us in the right direction. This book should be required reading for every parent.

Donna Cansfield - Past President Canadian School Boards Association, Past President Ontario School Boards Association and presently a Trustee with the Etobicoke Board of Education

This is a wonderful book to hand to parents of young children, who are eager to have them do homework as early as grade one. By showing parents how learning is a full time experience, not just something that happens at school, and that we can fully support learning at home, we are able to "reach and teach" throughout the student's day in a more meaningful way.

All the parents I have shared this book with have had positive, enthusiastic comments to make about it. Well done!

Ann-Marie Pattenden - Teacher

Your advice to support children's important learning by acknowledging, reinforcing, celebrating and rewarding is so true! The Learning Labs are open ended, allowing for input from child or parent. Your agreement of writing development and ways to encourage it is very easy to implement in homes.

The hints for sharing parental knowledge about their children with the school staff are helpful. I'm pleased to see your delineation of what topics to address with the principal and what to discuss with the teacher.

Margaret Roberts - Principal, York Region Board of Education

Fascinating! As a parent with a "special needs" child this book is exactly what we need. Teaching our children as "we were taught" can sometimes be a very frustrating experience for everyone. This book's perspective is of tremendous value to all parents. Focusing not on teaching but on understanding how our children understand makes perfect sense!

Excellent coverage of every aspect of the child's life and the opportunities that exist to "teach" in everyday life.

Melanie Dornan - President

Smart From the Start is an invaluable book for parents. It provides a comprehensive guide about how our children learn and how we as parents, can provide the necessary tools to make effective learning links between home and school, and in preparing our children for their future endeavours.

Jill Maar - Teacher/Parent

De-mystifying the learning experience. I found the approach of the parent as a teacher, tied in with the acknowledgement that we are all teachers and learners, an excellent one. Varied use of pictorial symbols to supplement the reading makes for quick and easy retention of ideas.

Barbara Rodrigoe - Montessori Co-ordinator

Smart From the Start

Making the most of your child's learning

Janet Millar Grant

Vicky L. Hopton

Susan Fleury Pearson

Helene Pfeiffer

Gateway Books
Brampton, Ontario

To Alexis and Conor Grant, two wonderful learners who teach me everyday
and who have truly been Smart From the Start.
Janet Millar Grant

To Tom and Jean Hopton, my first teachers, who gave me a Smart Start in life.
Vicky Hopton

To my first teachers, Ivan and Eugenia Dalyk-Husak, who will always continue
to be a source of learning for me.
Helene Pfeiffer

To our six special children, Joanna, Shari, David, Robert, Wesley, and Laura,
who have been my inspiration.
Susan Pearson

Acknowledgements

Thank you to our friends and family who supported and encouraged our efforts.

Special attention goes to Rolf Pfeiffer for his author pictures and outstanding cover.

An extra special thank you to the collective efforts of the author team who each willingly shared their insights, expertise and humour with each other to make this project a reality.

Published by Gateway Books
6-295 Queen Street East, Suite 417
Brampton, Ontario, Canada L6W 4S6
Phone: 905-456-2993
Fax: 905-456-8128
Internet: vhopton@edu.yorku.ca

Canadian Cataloguing in Publication Data
Grant, Janet Millar
Smart From the Start: Making the most of your child's learning / Janet Millar Grant, Vicky L. Hopton,
Susan Fleury Pearson, Helene Pfeiffer
1. Education 2. Parent/Child Relationship 3. Learning 4. Millar Grant, Janet 5. Hopton, Vicky
6. Pearson, Susan 7. Pfeiffer, Helene

ISBN: 0-9683552-0-X

Cover Design: Rolf J. Pfeiffer, Graphic Design
Editor: Inara Jenkins
Book Layout: Teresa Hamilton, Heydon Graphics

Printed in Canada

TABLE OF CONTENTS

TABLE OF CONTENTS

PART IV

LEARNING LINKS BETWEEN HOME AND SCHOOL

PART V

LEARNING AT SCHOOL

PART VI

LEARNING IN THE FUTURE

APPENDICES

INTRODUCTION

What have you learned lately?

Learning is much more than a stack of books. It is definitely more than what takes place in institutionalized locations such as schools and colleges. In fact, you were involved in learning long before you even entered school and you continue to learn as you grow up and move out of school. Why, at the very least, you learn to cope with getting older.

Learning is a process that involves gathering information, gaining skills, considering alternatives, making choices and acting on those choices. These choices in turn leads to gathering more information, gaining new skills, considering diverse alternatives, making different choices—and so on and so on....

Learning is an integral part of your life, even though it may not be very **apparent** to you. Which brings us to consider learning as it occurs in a most important phase of your life. Please pardon the pun and read on.

You are "A-Parent-ly" Learning

One of the major areas of learning for you as an adult occurs when you choose to take on the task of caring for a child. **ZAP**—you are immediately immersed in learning to be a parent. As a caregiver, you want to provide the best start possible for your child. As a parent, you have the most significant role to play in making your child *SMART FROM THE START*. In fact you, as a parent, become your child's first teacher. You are responsible for getting him started in the world as a learner.

Rather a daunting task you might say. Indeed, learning can be seen as a rather awesome responsibility if you try to think of it as one task. However, when you take time to consider learning as a total concept made up of many, smaller components, the responsibility becomes more manageable. Also, there are resources that can help you out.

TA-DAH! Which naturally brings us to this book. ***SMART FROM THE START*** focuses on what you can do to support learning at home. Through practical suggestions and tips you will be able to identify how your child learns and how you can be involved in supporting your child's learning.

Does parent involvement make a difference? **YES INDEED!** Research tells us that children learn better when parents are involved.

SMART FROM THE START will help your child to be a successful learner by:

✔ helping you to understand what learning is and how to recognize it when you see it

✔ exploring simple ways in which you can support learning at home

✔ recognizing and reinforcing your role as your child's teacher

✔ describing a selection of learning opportunities for you to enjoy with your child

✔ helping you to understand how learning at home relates to learning at in school

✔ providing you with tips for interacting with schools

✔ providing you with ways that you and your child can celebrate and enjoy learning

✔ offering you a basic framework or understanding that will help you to organize and enrich a variety of learning experiences for your child

Speaking of organization, **how is this book organized?**

The focus of this book is on learning. Learning is a continual process that requires the learner to be actively involved in making connections between old and new learning. It also demands that the learner take time to collect her thoughts and consolidate what she has learned.

We would like you to be an active participant as you explore this book. We invite you to investigate ideas about learning and to think about learning. To that end, we have included pages called **LEARNING LOGS** which are designed to assist you in your personal reflections. To help you in consolidating your learning, we have also summarized each part of the book in an acrostic as well as a flow chart.

SMART FROM THE START is a guide for you to **maximize your child's learning**. You can open the book at any point, and select information and activities about learning that is relevant to you and your child.

looks at you as a learner, you as a teacher and the nature of learning. You will be encouraged to think of yourself as a learner, to consider what helped you to learn, how you learned and what learning feels like and looks like.

allows you to be able to recognize learning at home and identify ways to support learning. Strategies will be provided for you to create a productive learning environment at home as you monitor, support and encourage learning.

provides you with a selection of specific suggestions and activities that will enrich your interactions with your child. It is intended to help you can pick and choose which activities will best suit the needs of your child. By involving your child in such rich learning opportunities you will be able to support your child's learning successes.

links learning at home to learning at school. It examines how your child learns language, mathematics, science and other subjects both at home and at school. Lists of our favourite books are also included.

You will learn how your expertise is valued at school. It will show you the similarities between learning at home and learning at school. A series of frequently asked questions are presented to address common concerns you may be facing.

In the final section of the book, we'll take a look into our crystal ball to look at how a **SMART START** will support **SUCCESS** in the future. You will explore what your child will need to learn, and how to learn, in the years to come.

Throughout *SMART FROM THE START* we hope you take a chance and try some activities on for size. We know that learning cannot be prescribed and that you will need to adapt our suggestions to suit you. Learning doesn't come in a kit, but it does come in the minds of all of us.

Janet Millar Grant

Helene Pfeiffer

Vicky L. Hopton

Susan Fleury Pearson

A Message from the Authors

We have been learners all of our lives. Our experiences as parents, teachers, school administrators, consultants, workshop leaders and university instructors have provided us with opportunities to continue to refine and deepen our understanding of the crucial role that **LEARNING** plays in all of our lives.

We feel we've been fortunate to have been able to see the power of learning at close quarters. Enthusiasm and commitment to learning have woven common threads in each of our lives. We have always relished opportunities to share anecdotes about learning and analyze the components of the learning process. You could say we were charter members of *The Learning Obsessed*!

In fact, this book was born during one of our ongoing chats about learning around a lunch table. We wanted to share our enthusiasm for learning with a wider audience. Let's face it, our immediate family members were beginning to tire of our incessant stories about our students! In exploring our initial germ of an idea, we recognized that our lives as "professional learners" had been shaped **right from the start** by our parents. So it was that we elected to design our book to reach other parents.

We believe that **LEARNING IS EVERYWHERE**. It is exploding all around us in an exciting process that allows us to explore an endless realm of possibilities through a wide variety of experiences. (For instance, we have learned a great deal in writing this book—WOW!). To capture the spirit of learning, we have made deliberate choices about the style and format of our book. We have tried to present our information in a friendly way that is meant to mirror the fun and joy of learning. For the same reasons our text contains manageable chunks of information with light-hearted graphics. We want our readers to be inspired to enjoy learning and realize the potential for their children to be *SMART FROM THE START*.

Enjoy!

WHAT IS LEARNING?

Part
I

All of us, at some point in our lives, have had some experience as learners. So given this first hand experience, we should understand the process of learning. How exactly does one learn? What helps us to learn? Do we all learn the same way? Do we have any volunteers who want to explain this learning process?

Ahh—not seeing a rush of volunteers is understandable. In fact, most of us do not spend a great deal of time thinking about learning as a process. We are more conscious about learning as we begin acquiring a new task or skill, but we rarely indulge in analyzing what is involved in learning. We are most concerned with getting on with it!

That is exactly what this book wants to do—help you to "get on with it". In this case we want to help you understand the many ways that you can support the learning of your children. However, it is important for us to take a little bit of time to come to a basic understanding of what is involved in the learning process. Relax now, this will be relatively painless! Why, you probably have all of the necessary equipment close at hand. Take a few minutes and gather together the following:

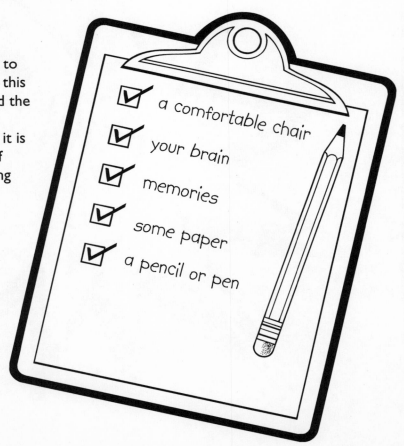

- ✓ a comfortable chair
- ✓ your brain
- ✓ memories
- ✓ some paper
- ✓ a pencil or pen

We presume that you located those items quite quickly. Make yourself comfortable and begin to think about a time when you had to learn something new. Perhaps it was a new game or sport or something required for your job.

An Activity For You

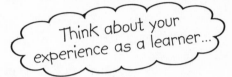

Think about your experience as a learner...

1 WHAT DID YOUR LEARNING LOOK LIKE?

Which words best describe what your learning looked like?

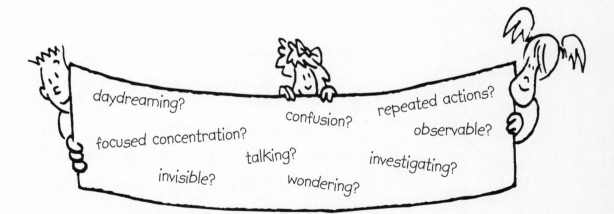

daydreaming?

confusion?

repeated actions?

focused concentration?

observable?

talking?

investigating?

invisible?

wondering?

2 WHAT HELPED YOU TO LEARN?

✔ Did you build on previous knowledge?

✔ Did you use specific resources, like a manual, a model etc.?

✔ Did you compare your current performance to past learning?

✔ What environment was needed to support your learning?

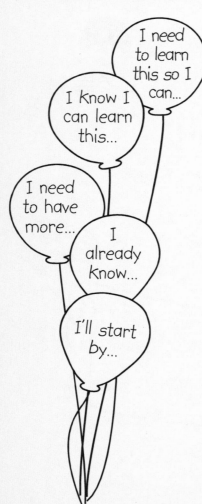

3 HOW DID YOU LEARN?

✔ Did you begin by learning one small skill or a larger concept?

✔ Did you learn in an orderly sequence of steps?

✔ Did you learn in isolation or with others?

✔ Did you learn slowly? Quickly?

✔ Did you learn your task all at once or in small steps?

✔ Did you have to try a few times to learn?

✔ Did you need to have the task presented to you in different forms?

✔ Were you actively involved in your learning?

✔ Did mistakes hinder or help your learning?

✔ Did you learn something that was useful to you?

✔ Did you receive feedback about your learning?

✔ Did you expect to be successful?

✔ Did you celebrate your learning?

4 **WHAT DID LEARNING FEEL LIKE?**

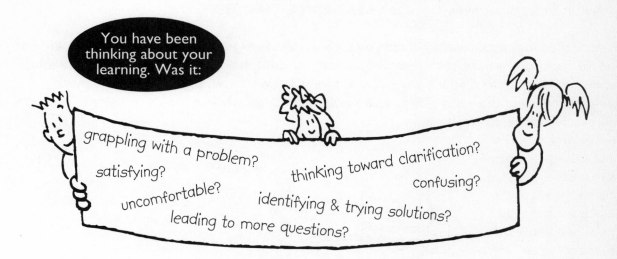

You have been thinking about your learning. Was it:

grappling with a problem?

satisfying?

thinking toward clarification?

confusing?

uncomfortable?

identifying & trying solutions?

leading to more questions?

 5 **WHAT DOES LEARNING LOOK LIKE?**

 Found a solution

Accomplished a task

 Discussed a concern

Answered a question

Raised a question

Resolved an issue

When you are involved in these types of activities, you are involved in learning!

As you considered the questions asked in the preceding pages, you were analyzing learning. You were, in fact, gaining experience as a **LEARNING THEORIST**.

Your reflections about what helped you to learn and how you learned are similar to what professional researchers have been examining in studies about learning. We are much more informed about learning today than we were in the days when we were "professional students". We are aware of the many differences among individuals when it comes to being successful learners. We are also more aware of the conditions that help us to learn. If we compare learning to making a balanced meal, we know that there are many ingredients that go into the mix to make a tasty, nutritious meal. In order to be successful learners, we need to include the following ingredients:

recipe

- ✔ other people
- ✔ a supportive environment
- ✔ high expectations
- ✔ real, relevant tasks
- ✔ immediate feedback
- ✔ opportunities to learn in a variety of ways
- ✔ opportunities to take ownership and responsibility

So we now know that you are indeed a **LEARNER** and that you are a fledgling **LEARNING THEORIST**. But are you a **TEACHER**? Sometimes we're uncomfortable with that word. We may be put off by the idea of what a teacher is. We may be alienated by personal experiences with teachers who were less than positive. However, take time to consider your experiences as a parent, particularly when you were dealing with your children as babies and toddlers. What kinds of things did you do?

✔ Did you provide a caring and supportive environment?

✔ Did you encourage your child to make first attempts at crawling, walking and talking?

✔ Did you accept her first attempts?

✔ Did you reward your child for "being close"?

✔ Did you model appropriate behaviors such as words, steps, etc.?

✔ Did you expect your child to learn to talk, to crawl, to walk?

✔ Did you give your child positive feedback by smiling, touching, etc?

✔ Did you let your child make mistakes?

✔ Did you let your child encounter tasks in different forms e.g. hearing oral sounds, conversations, songs, rhymes, stories?

✔ Did you offer words of encouragement?

✔ Did you expect your child to be an active or passive participant in her learning?

✔ Did you provide resources such as toys and books to support her learning?

✔ Did you observe your child learning?

✔ Did you make note of major milestones in her learning?

✔ Did you see your child making connections from previous learning to a new skill?

✔ Did you celebrate your child's successes in learning?

If you were able to answer yes to most of the above questions then you are indeed a **TEACHER**. And you thought that you only had to worry about being an effective parent!

Don't be intimidated by thinking of yourself as a teacher. In fact, you have assumed responsibility for the greatest teaching of all—helping your child to learn to walk and talk!

So, now that you realize how many skills you have developed in your various roles as a parent, learner, learning theorist and teacher, we think that you're ready for a pop-quiz. Don't panic! We wouldn't ask you to take this quiz if we didn't think you could be successful. After all, a sensitive teacher is always aware of the capabilities of the learner. **YOU CAN DO IT!**

First find a piece of paper. Jot down the following title: "**WORDS TO DESCRIBE LEARNING**". Or use the space we've provided.

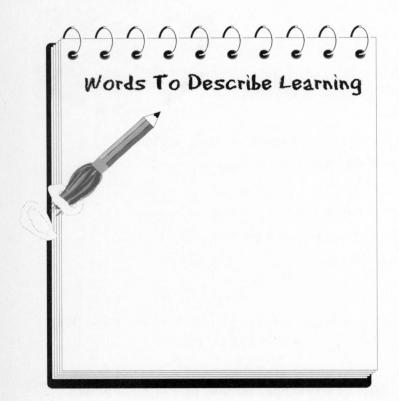

Words To Describe Learning

Given your personal experiences, what words could you list to describe learning? Think back to your earlier personal reflections about yourself as a learner. Think about the interactions you had with your young children as they learned to walk and talk. For the purpose of this quiz you may talk with someone else about possible words to include. In fact, we encourage you to do this because learning is very much an **interactive, collaborative** process. There—we just gave you two words to start your list. Now, start jotting . . .

. . . FIVE MINUTES LATER

How are you doing? Do you need to take a stretch? Do you need a snack? Do you need more light? Learning is a very **personal** process and we all have different **styles** of learning. OOPS—we just gave you two more words for your list!

When you have a list that you like, please move on to the next page.

L

LEARNING is a **LIFELONG** activity that occurs every day in many forms.

E

EXAMINE the many ways in which you learn.
Learning is unique to **EACH** individual.
Everyone has different **ELEMENTS** in their personal learning style.

A

ACCEPT the uniqueness of your learning style.
ANALYZE your strengths and needs in order to
AFFECT your learning in a positive way.

R

RECOGNIZE the **RESOURCES** that help you learn.

N

NURTURE your **NATURAL** curiosity through varied opportunities to explore and investigate.

Learning involves taking risks.
We explore, investigate and
experiment to solve problems.

Problem Solving

Natural

Learning is natural.
We all have an innate
curiosity. We want to learn.

Interactive

Learning takes place
through our interactions
with other people
and materials.

Purposeful

Learning answers real needs.

LEARNING IS...

Ongoing

Learning never stops.

Personal

Learning is personal.
We each learn in
different ways and at
different rates.

Making Meaning

Learning helps us make
sense of our world.

LEARNING LOG

Help your child to think about thinking.
RECORD your child's thoughts, curiosities, experiences, ideas, questions.

Your thoughts about:

✔ What did my child already know?

✔ What produced a sense of accomplishment?

✔ What is a good question?

✔ When do I lend a helping hand?

✔ How can I sustain interest?

✔ What next?

Now that you have read this section, jot down questions, ideas, thoughts and feelings you may have.

_____

_____

_____

_____

_____

_____

_____

_____

_____

_____

_____

_____

_____

_____

_____

_____

LOOKING AT
LEARNING AT HOME

Part
II

When you welcome a baby into your home, you spend countless hours watching every little movement he makes. With a burst of **new parent enthusiasm**, you begin to mark every milestone the baby reaches. For example, one of the first areas that you focus on is **PHYSICAL GROWTH**. You track each kilogram and each millimetre (or ounce and inch, as the case may be). You consistently monitor the baby's growth and ask questions about his progress.

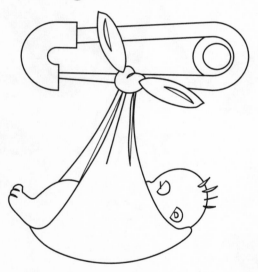

Congratulations

Rock-A-Bye Baby

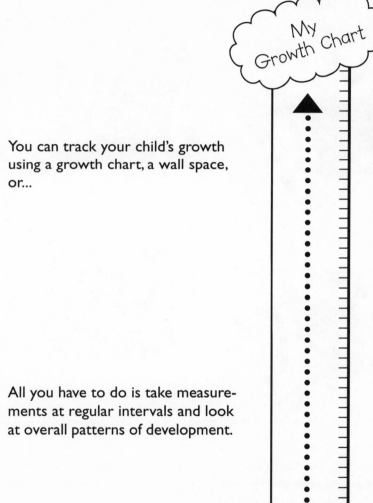

You can track your child's growth using a growth chart, a wall space, or...

All you have to do is take measurements at regular intervals and look at overall patterns of development.

You know when your child is growing PHYSICALLY.
There is ready evidence of growth:

- pants get too short

- there are holes in the toes of shoes

- clothes are too tight

Tracking your child's physical development over time allows you to gain insight into her consistent growth.

As your children grow and develop, you begin to see them reason and understand that when you cover your face with your hands, you do not really disappear totally. Or that when a toy is slightly out of reach they can manipulate their hands to grasp it. This is learning.

AS SHE EXPLORES HER IMMEDIATE ENVIRONMENT,
YOUR CHILD IS CONSTANTLY LEARNING.

Part
II

Not only does your child learn about his environment and how he can physically manipulate it, he is also learning about himSELF.

Just as your child goes through distinctive physical developmental phases, he goes through parallel stages of development in his socio-emotional growth.

1 SOCIO-EMOTIONAL DEVELOPMENT

Think about your child. As your child progresses along the developmental ladder, what do you notice in terms of his socio-emotional development? Which milestones has he passed through and which ones should you be looking out for...

✔ wanting to do things independently

✔ becoming responsible

✔ acting impulsively

✔ talking with adults

✔ finishing what he has started

✔ making friendships with both sexes

✔ seeking your praise and encouragement

✔ maintaining short-lived interests

✔ showing moody periods

✔ having difficulty sharing

✔ taking turns

✔ looking to you less for approval

✔ wanting to be a member of a group

✔ thinking about others

✔ imitating adults

S

Socio-emotional development: how a child learns to relate to others, the environment, and to the self. Key elements include values, attitudes, feelings, the understanding of right and wrong and self-esteem.

✔ needing more privacy

✔ recognizing the attitudes of others

✔ becoming secretive about personal thoughts and feelings

✔ wanting to be the leader

✔ criticizing adult actions

✔ analyzing personal behaviour

✔ testing the limits you set

Self-esteem is a key element of socio-emotional development.

Self-esteem grows as your child grows physically, but it also grows when children feel that they are loved and accepted.

You know that your child's self-esteem is growing when your child:

✔ eagerly takes on new challenges

✔ nurtures and is concerned about the feelings of others

✔ makes good choices

✔ displays flexibility and understanding

✔ distinguishes between right and wrong

✔ praises others

✔ knows that she will do the best that she can in order to be successful

✔ begins to positively influence others around her

✔ understands what she is good at

✔ accepts herself as she is

YOUR CHILD IS LEARNING ABOUT HIMSELF.

Monitoring your child's socio-emotional growth is also helping you to **LEARN** who your child is.

 ## 2 IS YOUR CHILD LEARNING?

Right from day one your child has been actively learning. AND it certainly never stops (much to parents' dismay at times!)

✔ How did she learn to ring the bell on the mobile?

✔ How did she learn to open those cupboard doors?

✔ How did she learn to sing that nonsensical song?

✔ How did she learn to share and play with friends?

Yes, your children are learning about what they can do physically and also about themselves and their relationships with others.

In addition, your child is experiencing important COGNITIVE or INTELLECTUAL development.

Just like the other areas of growth, intellectual development is also marked by milestones through which your child passes. Consider the following milestones as your child develops as a talker, a reader, a writer, a judge and a problem solver:

Problem Solving

is frustrated, gives up, asks for advice, attempts to solve the problem, understands that there is more than one way to solve a problem, uses appropriate problem solving strategies

Discriminating

focuses on appearance, explores, tries different solutions, transfers knowledge to new situations

Writing

scribbles, makes symbols, writes letters, writes words, creates a story

Reading

looks at a book, pretends to read, retells a story, reads using appropriate reading strategies

Talking

babbles, uses words, makes sentences, tells a story

 3 **RECOGNIZE LEARNING AT HOME**

Your child is immersed in learning at home. For you, it is a matter of becoming attuned to what learning is happening and how you can support the learning process.

listen, talk, watch

 Find ways to:

✔ **listen**
✔ **talk**
✔ **watch** ➡️ **as your child learns.**

  First, listen to your children talk about their learning.

Talk and listen to your children. What matters to them? What are their questions and concerns? What are they interested in? What are they excited about?

Children benefit from presenting ideas, concepts, and considerations to others. In order for them to do so, they need an audience. You can help support your child's learning by being a good audience, and that requires active listening.

Active listening requires focused attention on your child and what is being said. You need to know what you are listening for and should be able to retell what you've heard. Asking questions for clarification is part of active listening.

Active listening means focusing your attention on the child and maintaining eye contact. It means that you take the time to listen and respond to your child's dialogue in a meaningful way.

 Second, talk to your child about his learning.

Talking is a powerful tool for learning. As we talk, we process and clarify ideas and our thoughts and actions become clearer. As your child talks about his day, the learning that has occurred, and plans for tomorrow, he is processing his learning and preparing for learning to come.

You can support your child in learning by talking with him about...

- ✔ specific learning experiences
- ✔ patterns of learning
- ✔ future plans for learning

Ask your child questions about his learning.

Find out what he is doing at school, what and how he is learning, and upcoming areas of study.

Talking Tips
- ✔ Capitalize on the times that your child normally likes to talk..
- ✔ Identify her interests and initiate the talk from her area of interest.
- ✔ Allow her to direct the conversation.

"What did you learn in school today?"
"How is that important?"
"What do you know now?"
"How do you know that you have learned?"
"What do you want to know?"
"How can you show the learning?"
"What does that tell you about your learning?"
"What will you learn next?"

As you ask questions, your child will have to reflect on his learning, and think about his learning in a focused way. As he answers your questions, he will develop an understanding of how he learns. Learning about how he learns is the most important skill your child can develop.

Third, keep watching your child.

Continue to observe your child in order to recognize when he has reached a new milestone in his development.

LOOK for patterns of behaviour that appear consistently over time.

You can track this development in some sort of journal, log or memory book, or use a calendar or chart.

A busy parent doesn't have much time for keeping
a memory book for each child.
Try recording the milestones on a calendar and then look
back for patterns of growth.

LOOKING AT LEARNING AT HOME

4 CREATE A LEARNING EXPERIENCE AT HOME

Begin with...

- ✔ attention to your child's basic needs
- ✔ a caring, safe atmosphere
- ✔ a focus on the individual
- ✔ opportunities to interact with materials and people

> The home can *be* a rich and exciting environment for learning.
> Challenge your child to look for learning everywhere in his environment.

Add the following:

- ✔ a designated "learning space" for your child
- ✔ materials for learning, such as books, writing implements, computer equipment, software
- ✔ a variety of learning experiences—field trips, events...
- ✔ opportunities to talk about learning
- ✔ varied sources of print and numbers
- ✔ opportunities to work alone and with others

Welcome to our Quality Learning Environment

WANTED

YOU!

reward!

YOU are the most influential person in your child's learning.

By modeling learning yourself you are showing that you value the same characteristics in your child.

Has your child seen you:

listening?	questioning?	talking?	co-operating?
directing?	problem solving?	probing?	motivating?
taking risks?	celebrating learning?	testing alternatives?	playing?

Develop the LOUD THINK habit talking about your learning out loud.

✔ **Talk about yourself as a learner.**

✔ **Talk about problem solving.**

✔ **Demonstrate initiative.**

when I am solving a problem I find it helps to make a list of things I know.

LOOKING AT LEARNING AT HOME

Part II

You can help your children see their learning and celebrate their learning successes.

A great place to start is to help your children know more about themselves as learners by having them think about and talk about . . .

- ✔ what they know
- ✔ what they want to know
- ✔ how they will try to find out
- ✔ how they will learn *best*
- ✔ problems they face . . .

LOOKING AT LEARNING

- ✔ I learned that I . . . .
- ✔ I already know that . . .
- ✔ I re-learned that I . . .
- ✔ I was supposed to learn that . . .
- ✔ I faced these obstacles in learning . . .
- ✔ I am curious about this question . . .
- ✔ I plan to . . .

MONITORING LEARNING

- ✔ I used to think that all birds can fly but now I know penguins don't
- ✔ I'm still confused about . . .
- ✔ I do my *best* work when . . .
- ✔ I can't seem to learn when . . .
- ✔ I wish I had more time to . . .
- ✔ I think my work is . . .

> As your child matures, invite her to take on the task of tracking learning through a personal learning log, calendar or diary.

5 WHAT LEARNING SHOULD YOU SUPPORT AND ENCOURAGE?

There is only so much time in the day and at some point you have to make some decisions. What learning is **important** learning. What should you support and what should you leave alone?

Important learning processes include:

- ✔ risk-taking
- ✔ taking responsibilities
- ✔ getting involved in learning
- ✔ being motivated learners
- ✔ solving problems
- ✔ learning lifelong
- ✔ owning learning

How to support and encourage...as a parent, parents, family, extended family...

When you see **IMPORTANT LEARNING** taking place, support your children by...

✔ ACKNOWLEDGING that your child is developing new abilities

✔ REINFORCING their importance to the child's learning and development

✔ CELEBRATING progress toward constantly increasing learning and

✔ REWARDING achievements!

How you acknowledge, reinforce, celebrate and reward your child's learning will influence how your child feels about her achievements and if she will be willing to continue learning or try something new. Because you are an important person in your child's life, she will be concerned about how you react to her learning. Even adolescents, who often appear not to need their parents approval, will thrive on the attention you give to their efforts.

Consider praise. There are many ways that you can tell your child that his efforts are valuable and worthwhile. You can give this message to your child through:

WORDS

✔ terrific
✔ you can do it
✔ I have faith in you
✔ super
✔ give me five
✔ what a great try
✔ fantastic

✔ yes
✔ you're the best
✔ excellent
✔ wow
✔ you are special
✔ fabulous
✔ good for you

GESTURES

✔ a smile
✔ a pat on the back

✔ a nod
✔ a hug

CELEBRATIONS

✔ tell an aunt
✔ tell a best friend
✔ write a pen pal
✔ create a display
✔ begin a scrapbook

✔ e-mail a cousin
✔ telephone a grandparent
✔ post work on the fridge
✔ take a photograph
✔ create a tee-shirt

REWARDS

✔ allow your child to choose a new activity to do with you

✔ together, buy new tools (markers, paints) to be used in future learning experiences

✔ extend the learning through another experience, e.g. watch the movie of the book your child just finished reading.

Remember to make rewards that will support future learning.
Encourage your child to learn for the experience and for the love of learning
rather than for the reward itself.

Now you should have a much clearer picture of what LEARNING is.

It is time to
introduce you to
another key word:

 PLAY

PLAY = LEARNING

Play and learning go hand in hand.

Play is how children learn. Creative play is what children do best.

VALUE IT! ENCOURAGE IT!

Play is how children begin to make sense of the world.

Children learn through **PLAY** by making connections to what they already know. **PLAY** allows them to make new connections. **PLAY** is practice for real life.

During play children:

✔ experiment	✔ listen	✔ take risks	✔ assume roles
✔ test ideas	✔ communicate	✔ invent	✔ solve problems

CREATIVITY is another key element in the learning process.

 6

IS YOUR CHILD CREATIVE?

Does your child . . .

imagine?	tell stories?	draw?	paint?
write?	dance?	experiment?	build?
sculpt?	cook?	invent?	investigate?
play?			

 7

FOSTER CREATIVITY

Consider:

✔ How you can be involved by talking with and listening to your children.

✔ How often you ask questions about their play/learning.

✔ How you present yourself as a learner, a creative person, someone who plays.

✔ The environment for learning that you have in your home.

✔ The materials that you provide to stimulate and support creative play and/or learning.

Provide a wide variety of creative materials and allow your child time and freedom to explore and build with these materials.

Ensure that the materials you provide foster creativity and relevant learning. Look for materials that allow for a great deal of input and interpretation by the child.

Avoid relying heavily on activities such as colouring books which limit a child's creative expression.

8 EXAMINING LEARNING AT HOME

- a safe, supportive environment

- children interacting with people and materials

- parents taking an active role in developing and supporting learning

- parents modeling learning

- parents talking about learning

- parents and children celebrating learning

L

LOOK for **LEARNING** opportunities at home. **LOOK** at your children as **LEARNERS**. Support important, significant **LEARNING**. **LISTEN** to your children talk about **LEARNING**. Talk about yourself as a **LEARNER**.

E

ESTABLISH a caring, productive learning **ENVIRONMENT**. **ENCOURAGE** your children to use their initiative and to take risks. Foster play and creativity to **ENSURE** quality learning. Consider your children's interests and what they are **EXCITED** about.

A

ACKNOWLEDGE your children's developing **ABILITIES**. Encourage them to be **ACTIVE** participants in learning. **ALLOW** them to be **ACCOUNTABLE** for their actions. Ensure that you show your **APPROVAL** for their achievements and willingness to be involved in learning. **AVOID ACTIVITIES** that limit your children's creative expression.

R

RECOGNIZE the unique contributions of your children. Provide opportunities for them to assume **RESPONSIBILITIES** within your family. **REINFORCE** the importance of learning and **REWARD** your children's achievements.

N

NURTURE your children by taking care of their basic **NEEDS** for physical, emotional, and social stability. **NEGOTIATE** with them to set relevant learning goals for them to reach. **NOTE** your children's progress.

Whole Person

Learning involves the whole person—the physical, socio-emotional and intellectual development.

Recognizing Learning

Learning is recognized through observation, questioning, talking and listening.

LEARNING AT HOME IS...

Learning Environment

Learning requires a caring, supportive environment that values play and creativity.

Role of the Parent

Learning is modelled by parents. A child's learning is monitored through talking with and listening to your child.

LEARNING LOG

Help your child to think about thinking.
RECORD your child's thoughts, curiosities, experiences, ideas, questions.

Your thoughts about:

✔ What did my child already know?
✔ What produced a sense of accomplishment?
✔ What is a good question?
✔ When do I lend a helping hand?
✔ How can I sustain interest?
✔ What next?

Now that you have read this section, jot down questions, ideas, thoughts and feelings you may have.

_____
_____
_____
_____
_____
_____
_____
_____
_____
_____
_____
_____
_____
_____
_____
_____

LEARNING AT HOME WITH LEARNING LABS

Part III

LAB #1 COOKING UP A STORM

1. ON YOUR MARK...

Cooking experiences will allow you to foster the following:

- ✔ following directions
- ✔ measuring, counting, ordering, estimating
- ✔ reading
- ✔ organizing, planning
- ✔ telling time
- ✔ making judgements, decisions, predictions
- ✔ developing awareness of good nutrition, safety, healthy habits such as washing hands
- ✔ teamwork, co-operation
- ✔ growth in self esteem

2. GET SET...

Think about when, where and how you will cook...

- ✔ Snoop through your cookbooks, pick a recipe.
- ✔ Locate the ingredients or the substitutes which may work.
- ✔ Prepare all your utensils.
- ✔ Prepare the space.
- ✔ Make sure you have the time.

When getting ready consider your child as a cook...

✔ Is this a first experience or is my child quite competent in the kitchen?

✔ Will my child be challenged and excited or will this be frustrating and too complex?

✔ What is my role—how much input do I have to give? How much is too much?

✔ Have we explored new options? Cooking can be a great time to look at recipes from different cultures and to try something completely new.

✔ Have I thought about some changes I may need to make for the special needs of my child?

Involve your child in the experience through questions:

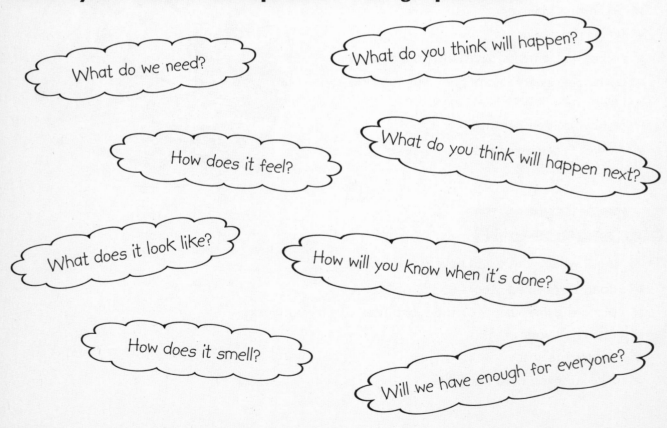

What do we need?

What do you think will happen?

How does it feel?

What do you think will happen next?

What does it look like?

How will you know when it's done?

How does it smell?

Will we have enough for everyone?

Good Questions Build Good Habits of Thinking

REMEMBER

A cooking experience does not need to involve the oven. Making a sandwich, a salad or a drink is just as valuable an experience for you and your child.

Make sure that all hands are washed before you begin.

3. GO...

The perfect recipe for cooking with your child.

- ✔ Pick a recipe.
- ✔ Locate the ingredients.
- ✔ Prepare the space.
- ✔ Find the ingredients and tools.
- ✔ Encourage your child to use a variety of kitchen tools such as graters, choppers and grinders.

cont'd

✔ First you do it.

✔ Then you give your child a try.

✔ Into the oven it goes.

✔ Clean up.

✔ The grand finale—tasting the fruits of your labour.

Consider different ways of involving your child in daily kitchen activities. Can they help while you are preparing a meal? Consider asking your child to:

Older children can be much more involved in the kitchen. They can:

✔ plan a weekly meal

✔ make their own lunches

✔ try recipes which are more complex

✔ help out in the kitchen on a daily basis

Involve all your children in cooking activities—sons and daughters alike!

EXPERIMENT

Not all recipes are for eating. For a change of pace, try the recipe for GOOP that follows on page 54.

Set the table to reflect the menu:

Consider...

- ✔ How many will be eating?
- ✔ Who will be eating? (setting up for a toddler will look different than setting up for an adult).
- ✔ What we will be eating?
- ✔ Where we will be eating?
- ✔ Which utensils we will need (plates, bowls, glasses, cups, napkins, chopsticks)?

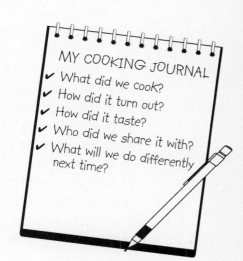

MY COOKING JOURNAL
- ✔ What did we cook?
- ✔ How did it turn out?
- ✔ How did it taste?
- ✔ Who did we share it with?
- ✔ What will we do differently next time?

SHARE   Share with parents, siblings, friends, neighbours, teachers...

RECORD   Start a cooking diary with your child. Keep it in a folder on your computer or in a spiral notebook...

CELEBRATE LEARNING...

- ✔ Take a taste test.
- ✔ Deliver samples to family and friends.
- ✔ Serve the results.

TO TRY LATER...

- ✔ Make a recipe collection.
- ✔ Tape (audio or video) the process.
- ✔ Dramatize a "cooking show".
- ✔ Try the recipes on the following pages.

RECIPE FOR GOOP

This mixture allows children to enjoy the sensation of squeezing something beautiful from a bottle. The design can be enhanced by adding sparkles, beads sawdust, shells etc.

Ingredients:
2 cups flour
1/2 cup salt
1/4 cup sugar
1 1/2 cups water
1 tsp paint

- Mix the flour, salt and sugar.
- Add the water very slowly until you have reached a consistency that will allow to be squeezed from bottle.
- Add the paint for colour.
- Pour the mixture into a squeeze bottle - a recycled ketchup, mustard or small detergent bottle.
- Squeeze the mixture onto construction paper, cardboard or fingerpaint paper.
- Add details such as sparkles, shells . . .
- Allow to dry.

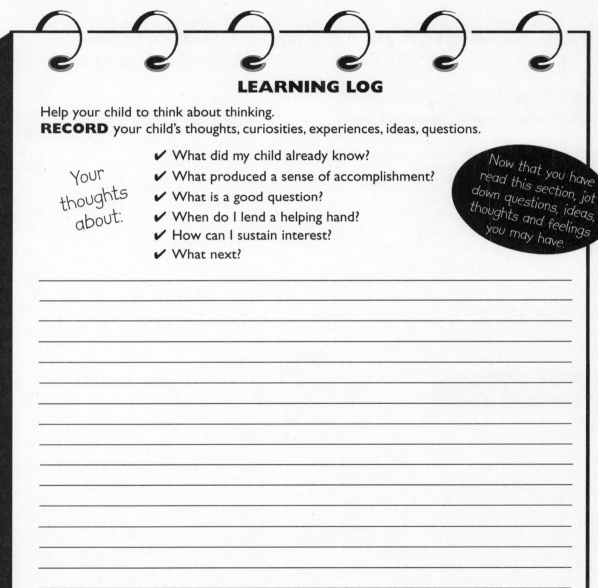

LEARNING LOG

Help your child to think about thinking.
RECORD your child's thoughts, curiosities, experiences, ideas, questions.

Your
thoughts
about:

✔ What did my child already know?
✔ What produced a sense of accomplishment?
✔ What is a good question?
✔ When do I lend a helping hand?
✔ How can I sustain interest?
✔ What next?

Now that you have read this section, jot down questions, ideas, thoughts and feelings you may have.

LAB #2 A STEP IN THE RIGHT DIRECTION

1. ON YOUR MARK...

Outdoor experiences will allow you to foster the following curiosities, actions and habits of mind:

- ✔ planning
- ✔ communicating
- ✔ appreciating and caring for the environment
- ✔ investigating, researching
- ✔ recording
- ✔ presenting findings

Planning a nature walk. This outline will work for most trips.

2. GET SET...

Things to bring:

- ✔ camera
- ✔ binoculars
- ✔ compass
- ✔ bags for collections
- ✔ recording devices
- ✔ snack
- ✔ friends
- ✔ raincoat

Does this ladybug look like the one we saw before?

As you enter your child's world, link what you already know to what you see, hear, smell, think, and feel. Making connections grows brain dendrites.

It's not how many trips or how many facts your child memorizes; rather, it's exploring questions, thoughts and feelings that results in depth of learning.

Take time to:

✔ discover what interests your child deeply

✔ uncover your child's thought processes

✔ understand what your child values and appreciates

This awareness will guide what you decide to collect and record.

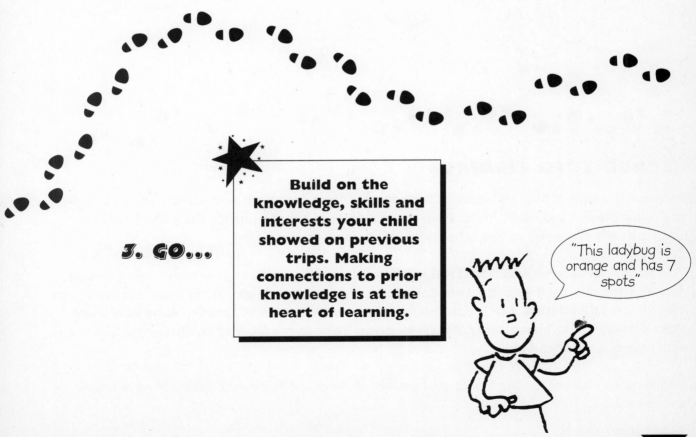

3. GO...

Build on the knowledge, skills and interests your child showed on previous trips. Making connections to prior knowledge is at the heart of learning.

"This ladybug is orange and has 7 spots"

Many children are interested in things that they find in their natural surroundings.

Press leaves and wild flowers in a discarded telephone book.
or
use folded wax paper pressed with a warm iron.

RECORD YOUR FINDINGS

Purchase the type of photo album that has adhesive pages protected with a clear film that allows you to lift the film and insert items. Many albums come in a three-ring format with removable pages that will allow you to add other types of pages or envelopes.

This album can become a **LEARNING LOG** that easily allows you to save small findings, notes, drawings and photos. If your child has collected leaves, preserve them, identify the trees and place them in the **LEARNING LOG**. You should revisit sites a number of times to observe changes, make drawings, take photos and collect new items. Refer to the **LOG** to compare new findings with previous observations.

Find ways to make recording fun. Special pencils, stickers and fancy note pads add novelty and excitement.

Show your child that you care about the environment. Take a bag for litter and be careful not to damage the surroundings.

Investigate the soil, bark, insects, common weeds, animal prints or droppings.
Small plastic bags are handy to store loose items.
Bark rubbings are fun, safe and easy to do.

Take time to look at the album together. Talk about the learning that has occurred. Include a note about the weather. Show it to others. Have a special place to keep it where you will revisit it often.

Display your collection. A dish of acorns or a potpourri of needles and cones values nature and shows and an appreciation for your world. Experiment with preservatives. Try coating acorns with clear nail polish or hair spray. What do you notice in a few days? Take discoveries to school to share with others.

POINTS TO PONDER

What new interests emerged? Future trips will evolve naturally. Perhaps an interest in an animal hole will lead to a discussion of the types of animals that live in the woods. Consider possible sources where you can research this information.

You are now encouraging your child to:

... ask questions

... investigate

... use technology? (cameras, compass)

... use research skills? (library, computer)

... reflect on learning

... collect and classify

... record in a variety of ways

... celebrate learning

... be a weather watcher

... respect and value the environment

... understand and practice the three R's

Reduce - Recycle - Reuse

CELEBRATE LEARNING...

✔ Record experience with photos, drawings.

✔ Create a nature scrapbook.

✔ Talk about your walk.

✔ Tell others what you saw, heard, felt.

TO TRY LATER...

✔ Design a weather station.

✔ Compose a hiking song, rhyme.

✔ Keep a weather log.

✔ Make rubbings of objects.

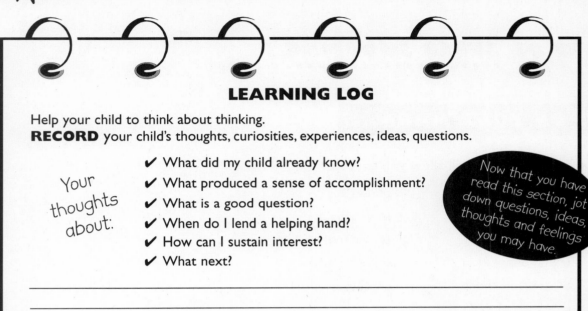

LEARNING LOG

Help your child to think about thinking.
RECORD your child's thoughts, curiosities, experiences, ideas, questions.

Your thoughts about:

✔ What did my child already know?
✔ What produced a sense of accomplishment?
✔ What is a good question?
✔ When do I lend a helping hand?
✔ How can I sustain interest?
✔ What next?

Now that you have read this section, jot down questions, ideas, thoughts and feelings you may have.

LEARNING AT HOME WITH LEARNING LABS

Part III

LAB #3 SUPER SHOPPING

1. ON YOUR MARK...

Shopping experiences will allow you to foster the following:

- ✔ organization
- ✔ reading
- ✔ identifying
- ✔ cataloguing
- ✔ making change
- ✔ decision making
- ✔ writing
- ✔ planning
- ✔ estimating
- ✔ budgeting
- ✔ classifying

GET SET...

Shopping requires planning. Children can learn the value of planning if you can model the different approaches towards a shopping experience. When you get ready to go shopping do you think about what you will shop for or do you just go to the store and let your mood guide you? When you go to the store consider whether you shop for all of the following at once:

- ✔ groceries
- ✔ soaps/detergents
- ✔ personal care items
- ✔ cooking utensils and tools
- ✔ clothing
- ✔ car maintenance products
- ✔ items for the home or garden

3. GO...

Shopping as you can see, can take on many dimensions depending on how you plan, what you intend to purchase and where you intend to go.

First things first!!!

To help your child plan and organized begin by compiling a shopping list. Think about how you compile your shopping list?

Do you:

✔ plan your meals and then make up your shopping list?

✔ scan the cupboards, identify what's missing and from this make your list?

OR

Is your shopping list a combination of these approaches?

MAKING A LIST

Look at flyers and coupons and consider how they will shape your shopping list and your shopping experience.

Grocery List
- bananas
- apples
- broccoli
- carrots
- celery
- onions
- mushrooms
- eggplant
- tomatoes

While creating a shopping list with your child, you are teaching her a valuable writing skill.

If you are the type of shopper who makes a list by first planning your meals for the week, think about how you could most meaningfully include your child in the process. Ask for your child's input and participation.

▶
- ✔ What do you think we should plan to eat this week?
- ✔ Would you like to try something new?
- ✔ Do we need to look through the cookbooks?
- ✔ Which ingredients do we have?
- ✔ Which ingredients do we need?

Or are you the type of shopper who scans the cupboards for missing items and creates a shopping list this way? Which one are you?

▶
- ✔ With which cupboard should we begin?
- ✔ Is there a specific order for looking through the cupboards?
- ✔ Is there a pantry, storage or basement cupboard we have to look through?
- ✔ Do we need to check the freezer?

Shopping lists are as unique as the individuals who write them. Some unique styles are listed:

- ✔ alphabetical order
- ✔ random order
- ✔ check off on a pre-determined list
- ✔ according to where items can be found in the store
- ✔ according to where items are stored in your home
- ✔ according to meals
- ✔ according to the stores being visited

CONSIDER BUDGETING

While creating your shopping list, think about the concept of budgeting. This is a perfect opportunity to involve your child in developing the real life skills required in money management.

While budgeting, you can talk about:

✔ establishing a budget
✔ estimating expenditures
✔ prices of items

✔ the importance of comparative shopping
✔ shopping within a budget

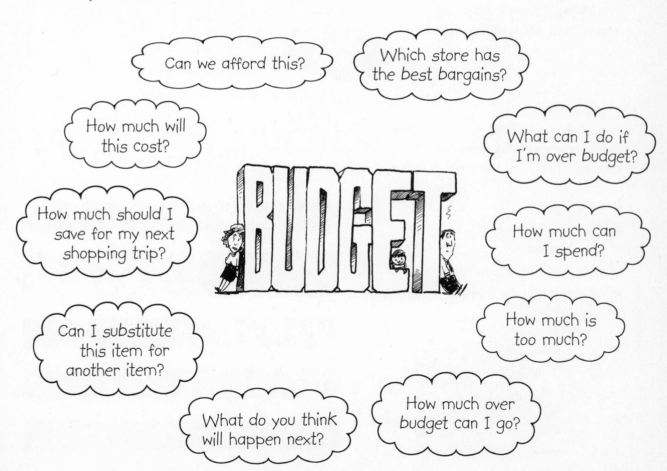

AT THE STORE ASK YOUR CHILD:

✔ Where shall we go first?

✔ How much time do we have?

✔ What do we need to buy first?

✔ How can we best organize our time and travel needs?

✔ Do we need to take our own shopping bags or boxes?

✔ Do we need cash, credit cards, or shall we use the bank machine or interact?

Putting the shopping into the shopping list...

Where to first?

✔ the bakery section

✔ dairy foods section

✔ fruits and vegetables

✔ the deli counter

The layout of the store and how you organize your shopping list will dictate how you approach your shopping experience. Why are there three different brands of paper towels?
While choosing items on the shelf, help your child become familiar with:

✔ prices

✔ expiry dates

✔ brand names

✔ cost per unit

✔ environmentally friendly packaging

✔ hazard warning symbols

Are they all the same?

Do they have the same number of sheets per roll?

What is the price difference?

Is this made out of recycled paper?

Which is the most economic?

Making informed choices promotes critical thinking.

TO USE A CALCULATOR OR NOT TO USE A CALCULATOR

You may be hesitant in allowing your child to use a calculator when budgeting and shopping. Calculators are tools we use in daily life to conduct our calculations.

Some larger chain stores have calculators attached to their shopping carts for customers to use. This is a good opportunity for you to model the use of technology in our everyday lives. Encourage your child to use a calculator as a tool.

Each child should be encouraged to learn basic math skills such as adding and subtracting. Using the calculator will allow your child to develop additional skills which will be needed in the future as technology becomes more and more a part of their lives.

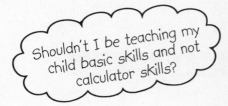

Shouldn't I be teaching my child basic skills and not calculator skills?

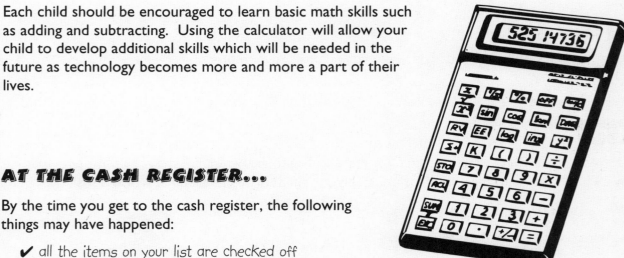

AT THE CASH REGISTER...

By the time you get to the cash register, the following things may have happened:

- ✔ all the items on your list are checked off

- ✔ additional items may have been added to your list

- ✔ a total is established using estimation

- ✔ a total is established using a calculator

Discuss with your child the systems in place at various stores for going through the cash. Some stores use a laser and bar code method. Other stores key in every price into the cash register. In some stores employees bag your purchases. In other stores customers bag their own purchases. Plan your shopping trips so that your child may have a variety of experiences at the cash register.

Paying the Cashier

Let your child make the decisions around paying the cashier when the total comes up. Allow them to think about the decisions they need to make.......

✔ How many bills shall I give?

✔ Which bills shall I give? A twenty or two tens?

✔ Can I make up the required change so that we don't have to break another bill?

✔ Did I receive the correct change?

Bagging

If you are at a store which requires the customers to bag their own purchases, use this opportunity to provide a valuable learning experience. Guide your child through making practical decisions.......

✔ How many bags or boxes will we need?

✔ What goes on the bottom of the bag?

✔ Shall we pack thinking about the way we unpack and store?

✔ Where will the frozen items go?

✔ Where will the eggs and other fragile items go?

BRINGING THE GROCERIES HOME...

For some reason or other, most children believe that the shopping experience is over once the groceries have been brought into the home. Have you noticed how they are nowhere to be found when it's time to put things into their proper spots? As adults we know that the shopping trip isn't over until all groceries are put away...now its time to ensure that our children develop this skill.......

Putting away groceries is a very personal experience unique to each household. Share with your child the method that you have developed. Allow children to modify and to make personal adjustments as they see fit.

Think about how you unpack the groceries in your kitchen...

Do you:

✔ Begin with the items which go into the freezer or refrigerator.

✔ Unpack according to the order of your cupboard.

✔ Put all the items on the kitchen table and then place them into the appropriate cupboards.

✔ Organize your cans and perishable items according to the expiry date.

✔ Randomly put items away as you pull them out from the bag.

Once all your groceries and shopping bags are put away, then finally your shopping trip is over....

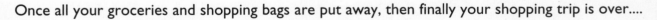

CELEBRATE LEARNING...

- ✔ Keep a bank account log.
- ✔ Develop a savings plan to buy an item.
- ✔ Plan a luncheon using groceries you bought.
- ✔ Initiate an allowance.

TO TRY LATER...

- ✔ Make a shopping list.
- ✔ Cut objects from flyers to make a list.
- ✔ Set up an imaginary store at home.
- ✔ Design invitations to the luncheon.
- ✔ Make a map of a store floor plan.
- ✔ Build a store using junk materials.

LEARNING LOG

Help your child to think about thinking.
RECORD your child's thoughts, curiosities, experiences, ideas, questions.

Your thoughts about:

✔ What did my child already know?
✔ What produced a sense of accomplishment?
✔ What is a good question?
✔ When do I lend a helping hand?
✔ How can I sustain interest?
✔ What next?

Now that you have read this section, jot down questions, ideas, thoughts and feelings you may have.

_____
_____
_____
_____
_____
_____
_____
_____
_____
_____
_____
_____
_____
_____
_____
_____

LAB #4 A TREK WITH TECHNOLOGY
. . . .

To most of us today, technology immediately means the use of computers. However in terms of general learning, technology has a much wider interpretation. For the young child, understanding technology begins with opportunities to build and construct.

1. ON YOUR MARK...

Using basis construction materials provides the child with opportunities to:

- ✔ observe
- ✔ explain
- ✔ question
- ✔ describe
- ✔ investigate
- ✔ compare
- ✔ explore
- ✔ design
- ✔ sort

- ✔ make predictions
- ✔ invent
- ✔ explore space
- ✔ make inferences
- ✔ solve problems
- ✔ make judgements
- ✔ order objects
- ✔ make patterns
- ✔ match

> In addition to developing small muscle skills and fine eye-hand coordination, construction tasks develop basic concepts such as: regular/irregular shapes, symmetry, area, circumference, directionality, counting, weighing, measuring, adding, subtracting, depth perception, spatial awareness,

2. GET SET...

SCIENCE, MATH and **TECHNOLOGY** are happening everywhere in a child's world. Is your child curious about why each snowflake is different? Does your child enjoy counting the members of your family? Does your child wonder why he goes up and you go down when you are on a tee-ter-totter?

Provide your child with opportunities to explore with a variety of construction materials. Let your child explore and learn about how things work. Encourage her to cut, hammer, screw, fasten, saw, balance, sort, order, weigh, measure and calculate.

Don't throw anything out. A child's imagination can take it and turn it into a valuable learning opportunity.

TECHNOLOGY EQUIPMENT

milk cartons	elastics	staplers
coat hangers	lids	broken appliances
tape	paper	nails
glue	hinges	bicycle wheels
egg cartons	jars	containers
jewellery		

3. GO...

TALKING ABOUT TECHNOLOGY

✔ DESCRIBE how you made your structure
✔ TELL me about what new things you discovered
✔ COMPARE this structure to your previous one
✔ What things MATCH in your structure?
✔ EXPLAIN how you made the base to support your structure

ADDING NEW CHALLENGES

Construction material can be supplemented with other items such as small vehicles, toy people etc. to create opportunities for imaginative play. Children can draw pictures of their structures, trace their structures, compose building directions, make a town, make a map...

As the child grows older, construction materials can include more complex building material, gears, pulleys, batteries, as well as wood working tools such as hammers, saws, screw drivers, etc.

The area of technology can also include opportunities to participate in the following tasks:

PICTURE IT

Experiment with photographic print making, *black and white photography*, produce audio and video tapes, stop action photography, trick photography.

TINKER WITH IT

Collect some material that children can experiment with by taking them apart and inventing new creations—broken clocks, buttons, knobs, dials, gears, wheels, pulleys.

DISCUSS IT

Involve your children in talking about issues:
- ✔ the value of technology in our world
- ✔ the social implications of technology
- ✔ ethics of technology
- ✔ freedom of speech on the Internet

COMPUTE IT

Children will *be living and working in a* world with computers. Support their understanding of how to use computers effectively by becoming informed about computer technology. Coordinate your efforts with what is happening in the schools.

Try these mathematical, scientific and technological tasks:

Indoors

✔ make a kite or paper plane

✔ hold balloon races

✔ take apart an old appliance

✔ learn to count in another language

✔ chart the weather on a calendar

✔ adopt a pet

✔ mix flour, water and food colouring to make playdough (see recipe on page 77)

✔ start a rock collection

✔ make an instrument

✔ bring in some snow and watch it melt

✔ make a house of cards

✔ start a coin collection

Outdoors

✔ put up a bird feeder

✔ plant a some scarlet runner beans

✔ look at the clouds

✔ observe the stars and the moon at night

✔ make a parachute

✔ observe some bugs

✔ look for patterns on houses, fences, walkways

✔ make list of all the forms of transportation that you see

✔ visit a construction site

✔ start a compost pile

✔ throw stones into a puddle

✔ collect and sort leaves

✔ organize a scavenger hunt: for geometric shapes, colours, plants. . .

✔ count the rings on a tree stump

In the Bathroom

- ✔ find things that will float/sink
- ✔ start a growth chart
- ✔ make bubbles
- ✔ fill different size containers in the tub
- ✔ mark the water level as your child gets in and out of the tub
- ✔ chart weight gain
- ✔ write messages on a steamy mirror
- ✔ find the most absorbent towel
- ✔ investigate how long it takes your family to use a tube of toothpaste
- ✔ make super bubbles using the recipe on page 78

In the Kitchen

- ✔ grow some bean sprouts or herbs
- ✔ sort the cutlery, laundry, toys . . .
- ✔ set the dinner table
- ✔ find all the kitchen tools that have a lever
- ✔ learn to use the timer on the stove
- ✔ put a thermometer up outside the kitchen window

CELEBRATE LEARNING...

- ✔ Photograph structures.
- ✔ Display structures.
- ✔ Design certificates of achievement.

TO TRY LATER...

- ✔ Enter an invention convention.
- ✔ Compose a construction journal.
- ✔ Design a new toy.
- ✔ Compose directions for making an item.

PLAYDOUGH RECIPE

Playdough is a wonderful material that can *be shaped, rolled, cut and moulded. It's flexibility* makes it a terrific stimulus for creative expression. It also makes a super gift or party favour - remember to include some basic cookie cutters with your playdough gift.

Ingredients:

I cup all purpose flour (250 ml)
1/2 cup salt (125 ml)
2 tbsp cream of tartar (25 ml)
I cup water (250 ml)
2 tbsp vegetable oil (25 ml)
food colouring (pasta food colourings will produce more intense, vibrant colours)

- Combine flour, salt and cream of tartar in a saucepan and stir together to blend.
- Combine water and oil.
- Stir the liquid into the flour and knead until smooth.
- Cook over medium heat until the mixture forms a ball, about 5 minutes.
- Turn out onto the counter and knead until smooth.
- Divide into two or three parts and add colour to each part.
- Store in a sealed container.

RECIPE FOR SUPER BUBBLES

The following mixture will allow you to create Super Bubbles that can be sources of great excitement and problem solving. As they set their own challenges and design the necessary tools, this activity allows children to be engaged in the creative discovery and application of science.

Ingredients:

6 glasses of water
2 glasses *clear* dishwashing detergent (JOY is the best)
1-4 glasses glycerine (available from the drugstore)

- Mix the above ingredients together. Using 4 glasses of glycerine is the best but in order to save the expense, you can use less.

- Create a variety of bubble makers using materials such as a coat hanger, string and funnels.

LEARNING LOG

Help your child to think about thinking.
RECORD your child's thoughts, curiosities, experiences, ideas, questions.

Your thoughts about:

✔ What did my child already know?
✔ What produced a sense of accomplishment?
✔ What is a good question?
✔ When do I lend a helping hand?
✔ How can I sustain interest?
✔ What next?

Now that you have read this section, jot down questions, ideas, thoughts and feelings you may have.

_____

_____

_____

_____

_____

_____

_____

_____

_____

_____

_____

_____

_____

_____

_____

_____

LAB #5 ARTISTIC ADVENTURES

1. ON YOUR MARK...

Engaging with the **ARTS** will allow you to foster the following:

- ✔ creating artistic expression
- ✔ representing what the child knows
- ✔ illustrating ideas
- ✔ expressing feelings
- ✔ communicating artistic messages
- ✔ displaying creations
- ✔ viewing art in a variety of forms
- ✔ reflecting on and responding to art
- ✔ developing skills to create, present and critique through the arts

2. GET SET...

What artistic materials could you have on hand?

✔ scarves	✔ props	✔ lummi sticks
✔ words	✔ literature	✔ beans in a jar
✔ poetry	✔ costumes	✔ tape recorder
✔ space	✔ mirror	✔ yarn, string
✔ music	✔ stories	✔ stapler
✔ paint	✔ instruments	✔ tape
✔ glue		

paper: poster, cardboard, corrugated, tissue, construction, wrapping

3. GO...

DANCING

- ✔ exercises
- ✔ a routine
- ✔ a series of movements,
- ✔ create 18 counts...

- ✔ a dance
- ✔ movement
- ✔ follow a routine
- ✔ filling space

floor sounds—beating, tapping, dragging, sliding, jumping, leaping, music, body sounds

MUSIC

Involve your children in exploring sound and rhythm.

- ✔ create a sound scape, song, score, melody, tune, lyrics, rhythm, instrumental piece
- ✔ record favourite sound
- ✔ make simple instruments (shakers, beaters)
- ✔ add "music" to favourite stories, poems or songs
- ✔ performing an instrument, singing
- ✔ listening to elements of music, its structure and form, sounds, instruments, (bought and made), voice, environmental, combination

VISUAL ARTS

- ✔ painting
- ✔ construction
- ✔ sketching
- ✔ sculpture
- ✔ printmaking

✔ communicating ideas and feelings through the creation of art

✔ understand and apply the elements, principles, concepts and terminology of art

✔ making meaning through interpretation

✔ making informed judgement about art by referring to the use of techniques and ideas as well as the aesthetic aspect of art—varied media, varied surface, perspective, colours

PICTURE PERFECT

Make a variety of drawing and colouring materials available including a variety of type and sizes of paper (lined, unlined, newsprint, construction, tag board, cardboard . . .)

Have many drawing tools available such as pencils, pens, markers, chalk, pastels, . . . Encourage your child to create original works of art.

Other ideas: trace hands, feet, body; make a mural; family portraits, make rubbings of objects.

PAINTING IMPRESSIONS

Provide non-toxic poster paint and many types of paper. Allow your child to explore the paint freely in picture making as well as other activities such as:

- ✔ *blobs (place paint in center of the page; fold over; press; unfold*
- ✔ *resist (make a crayon drawing; prepare a very diluted solution of paint; brush this diluted solution over the crayon drawing)*
- ✔ *painting with feathers, string, cord*
- ✔ *blow painting—drop paint onto a page, blow paint with a straw*
- ✔ *finger painting*
- ✔ *water colours*
- ✔ *print making—place paint on cut up vegetables or other objects; stamp object onto paper*
- ✔ *marble paper (see recipe on page 84)*

SCULPTURING

Allow children to create 3-D objects using clay, plasticine, boxes, construction paper, and paper maché.

Passionate about Paper

Have children design pictures and other items by using basic cut and paste. Other tasks to try could include paper tearing; mosaics; tissue paper overlays; papermaking.

RECIPE FOR MARBLE PAPER

Marble Paper allows your child to easily create a marvelous combination of colours that can be used in a variety of projects such as : wrapping paper, background paper for displaying drawings, poems, stories, or photos, end papers in self-made books, cover pages for self-made books, etc. In addition this experience provides opportunities to talk about some basic science principles.

Ingredients:

- 1 package unflavoured gelatin
- 2 cups hot (<u>not</u> boiling) water
- 2 cups cold water
- **oil based paint**—this can be recycled from home decorating or craft projects; it can also be purchased in small containers from hobby outlets.
- **plain white paper**—the weight and texture of writing paper—in sizes no larger than 8.5" x 11".

- Mix gelatin, hot and cold water together in a large shallow pan (foil roasting pans make good containers) to make a solution called SIZE.
- Drop a small amount of oil based paint on the surface of the size solution. The paint should float across the surface.
- Continue to add several colours (3-5).
- Move the colours around the surface of the size with a toothpick or by gently blowing across the surface.
- Place a sheet of paper onto the surface of the size. Lower the centre first then the sides.
- Remove the paper and let it dry.
- After creating a few pieces of marble paper, the colours can be skimmed off the surface of the size with a folded newspaper. New colours can then be added to the size.

 **DRAMA**

Take advantage of opportunities for spontaneous drama by providing dress-up materials; planning a puppet show; singing a song; reciting a poem; role playing; sharing favourite stories, nursery rhymes.

✔ create a tableau

✔ mime a story

✔ play a role from a favourite story

✔ dramatize an new ending to a song, story, poem

✔ make a sequence of statues

✔ create a puppet show

✔ dramatize a song, poem, story

Perfect Puppets

Puppets can be made from simple objects such as a spoon or feather duster. They can also be created from socks, paper bags, paper plates, foam pieces, paper maché, etc. (See pages 86-87 for more detailed suggestions).

CELEBRATE LEARNING...

✔ Display creations.
✔ Photograph creations.
✔ Make a video or audio tape.

TO TRY LATER...

✔ Create a gallery space in your home.
✔ Create memory quilt with photos of children's art.
✔ Compose directions for special projects.
✔ Create pop-up cards, pictures, books.
✔ Think of how you can use the creative materials suggested on page 88.

MAKING PUPPETS

Puppetry allows children to express themselves creatively in the construction and manipulation of the puppet. Telling stories with puppets reinforces oral language skills and capitalizes on the power of story as a basic element of successful learning. There are many types of puppets that can be created and used at home.

Finger Puppets

You can use fabric or paper to create Finger Puppets. Simply roll the material into a cylinder that can fit a finger. Stitch or tape into place and add details to create a character.

Walking Puppets

Make a character from paper or cardboard.
Cut out two circles near the bottom of the figure.
Insert your fingers to make the character walk.

Paper Bag Puppets

Allow children to manipulate the bag (a flat bottom style is best) in order to become familiar with the mouth location and movement. Decorate to create a character. Bags also be stuffed to create a 3 dimensional puppet.

Construction Paper Puppet

Fold a 21 cm x 31 cm piece of paper into thirds (with the long side at the top). Fold the bottom up to meet the top. Fold each of the two new top edges down to meet the centre crease. Use this basic shape to create an original character.

Paper Plate Puppet

Using construction paper or half a plate, create a pocket on top of a folded plate for the child to slide his/her fingers through as a controlling device.

Box Puppets

Two small boxes can be fastened together, creating a hinged mouth. A slit could also be made in one box to create a mouth.

Stick Puppet

A simple paper or cardboard figure can be attached to a rod. Styrofoam balls can also be attached to a rod and dressed to form a puppet.

CREATIVE MATERIALS

Ensure that this type of material is child-safe with all sharp edges and protruding pieces removed.

RECYCLED or FOUND MATERIALS

empty boxes
ribbon
cardboard
newspaper
thread
wire hangers
feathers
wallpaper samples/scraps
plastic bags
stones
leaves
picture frames
telephone books
wrapping paper
old gloves, mittens
old toys
pieces of foam, fur

paper towel/toilet paper rolls
string
fabric scraps
packing material
plastic containers, cutlery
pieces of foam
paper/foil plates
bottle lids
paper bags
shells
buttons
magazines
jewellery
greeting cards
sequins
wheels
empty spools

cans
yarn
foil
pieces of wood
styrofoam trays
popsicle sticks
beads
boxes
keys
seeds
jars
stamps
calendars
old socks, panti-hose
corks
springs
envelopes

broken appliances such as clocks, televisions, calculators, cameras, bikes etc.

COMMON HOME MATERIALS

cooking/baking ingredients	detergent	food colouring
nails, screws, fasteners	tin foil	wax paper
dried beans	noodles	nail polish
hair spray		

COMMERCIAL MATERIALS

plasticine	glue	masking tape
blocks	clay	poster paint
blank paper	markers	pens and pencils
picture books	novels	non-fiction books
building toys	pipe cleaner	fishing line

woodworking tools such as pliers, hammer, screwdriver, a simple vice

LEARNING LOG

Help your child to think about thinking.
RECORD your child's thoughts, curiosities, experiences, ideas, questions.

Your thoughts about:

- ✔ What did my child already know?
- ✔ What produced a sense of accomplishment?
- ✔ What is a good question?
- ✔ When do I lend a helping hand?
- ✔ How can I sustain interest?
- ✔ What next?

Now that you have read this section, jot down questions, ideas, thoughts and feelings you may have.

_____
_____
_____
_____
_____
_____
_____
_____
_____
_____
_____
_____
_____
_____
_____
_____
_____

LAB #6 COMPELLING COLLECTIONS

Collecting to Learn—start a collection to stimulate thinking and investigation.

1. ON YOUR MARK...

Collecting experiences and related follow-up activities allow you to foster the following:

- ✔ studying patterns and relationships
- ✔ organizing and analyzing
- ✔ recording in a variety of ways
- ✔ appreciating learning

2. GET SET...

Start with one collection that will bring excitement and challenge. When a child is truly interested, he will be naturally curious to want to find out more about it.

Discovering an Interest

- ✔ look through magazines and photo albums
- ✔ go for a walk
- ✔ visit your library
- ✔ talk about everyday happenings,
- ✔ investigate to see if a collection has been started

It is important to collect something that will sustain interest over time.

3. GO...

Share in the discovery process

✔ Explore the patterns, textures and colours in your collection.

✔ Discover patterns.

✔ Investigate similarities and differences.

✔ Sort in a variety of ways.

Help your child to sort and classify items by exploring criteria such as:

✔ size   ✔ colour   ✔ texture

✔ What do you notice about this collection?

✔ Tell me how you might group them.

✔ If I mixed them up, how else might you group them?

✔ How could we group them into three piles?

✔ What did you learn?

LEARN BY COLLECTING

Displaying collections in a variety of interesting ways provides opportunities for reliving experiences.

Provide feedback that:

✔ Encourages the child to generate questions.

✔ Allows them to have ownership of their work.

✔ Encourages them to pursue their exploration and investigation for extended periods of time.

POINTS TO PONDER:

✔ What new interests emerged? Would another collection foster new learning opportunities and build and extend previous learning.

✔ Connect collections to real life experiences.

✔ Are there collections in your home that your child can explore, sort and classify for a purpose? . . . such as buttons, old keys, greeting cards.

Learning must be experienced!

Share your learning with others.
Think of people that would find your collection interesting.
Discuss interesting ways to record your collection.

CELEBRATE LEARNING...

✔ Make a wall hanging made of material with velcro strips sewn across it. Attach velcro strip to pieces of your collection i.e. postcards, stamps, photos, pictures. Display collection on wall hanging.

TO TRY LATER...

✔ Make a stamp mobile.

✔ Make a model airplane, boat or other vehicle.

✔ Create shadow boxes from empty frames to display things like buttons, flowers, ...

✔ Decorate a special collection box.

✔ Find collections on the Internet.

✔ Join clubs such as Stamp Collecting.

LEARNING LOG

Help your child to think about thinking.
RECORD your child's thoughts, curiosities, experiences, ideas, questions.

Your thoughts about:

✔ What did my child already know?
✔ What produced a sense of accomplishment?
✔ What is a good question?
✔ When do I lend a helping hand?
✔ How can I sustain interest?
✔ What next?

Now that you have read this section, jot down questions, ideas, thoughts and feelings you may have.

_____
_____
_____
_____
_____
_____
_____
_____
_____
_____
_____
_____
_____
_____
_____
_____
_____
_____

LAB #7 FANTASTIC FRIENDSHIPS

Making friends is perhaps the most important skill your child will learn through out the school years. Getting along with others, empathy and effective communication will guide your child in successfully socializing with others. These are skills which are most critical to have so that children can grow up to be well adjusted and happy adults.

1. ON YOUR MARK...

In making friends and maintaining friendships, your child will develop the following critical skills and attitudes:

- ✔ empathy
- ✔ awareness
- ✔ patience
- ✔ effective communication
- ✔ cooperation
- ✔ collaboration

- ✔ problem solving
- ✔ reflection
- ✔ respect
- ✔ caring
- ✔ self-discipline
- ✔ responsibility

What is most important about developing friendships is that your child will feel included and a part of a peer community. This will allow your child to feel good about himself and about who he is.

2. GET SET...

There's a whole world of friends waiting for your child! Friends come in all shapes, sizes, skin colours, ages and abilities. Your child may choose to be friends with a wide variety of children. Or, as a parent, your role may be to help your child expand the circle of friends so that it includes all children. But first you need to think about your role and about the messages you may be sending to your child...

How you say it is as important as what you say.

As children try to make meaning from what you say, they read all the signs, even those that you are not aware of sending. Eighty percent of the meaning children pick up is not from what you say but how you say it.

The messages you may be sending your child through the way you say things may override the meaning you intended your child to get. In other words, we send messages not only through the words we use, but also by how we use them. The tone, volume and pitch of your voice along with the message you send through your body language can interfere with what your child understands you to be saying.

Consider how the following message can be perceived differently depending on which words you decide to emphasis when using pitch and volume in your voice:

✔ Alright, it's time to go to bed now.
> With no special emphasis, it is understood as a statement which has no particular urgency or underlying emotions attached to it.

✔ **Alright,** it's time to go to bed now.
> By emphasizing the first word, the underlying message becomes: "I need your attention immediately". The statement is no longer neutral.

✔ Alright, it's **time** to go to bed now.
> With an emphasis on the word **time,** the focus changes from a neutral statement to one which is more urgent in pointing out a deadline.

✔ Alright, it's time to go to **bed** now.
> With an emphasis on the word **bed,** the focus becomes the location. In this case, the location and the tone of voice in which it is identified may reveal the parents' frustration, fatigue or even anticipation of putting their feet up after a long day.

✔ Alright, it's time to go to bed **now**.
> With the emphasis on the word **now** a sense of immediacy comes across very clearly.

Think about the messages you may be sending to your child...

✔ Am I sending mixed messages by confusing what I am saying by how I am saying it?

✔ Is my tone of voice giving away what I am actually thinking and feeling?

✔ Is my body language sending messages I don't want it to send?

✔ Does the way I communicate interfere with what my child understands me to be saying?

What does sending clear messages have to do with your child developing friendships?

Consider how you react to your child's friends...
Are you...

- ✔ inviting?
- ✔ supportive?
- ✔ welcoming?

- ✔ caring?
- ✔ encouraging?
- ✔ hospitable?

Does what you say and how you say it, relate these sentiments?

Do you ensure that your home is an inviting and *safe* environment to which your child can bring friends?

Do you include friends in trips to the park or to the movies?

Do you encourage friends to share a family meal and to participate in sleep-over?

Do you make a point of getting to know your child's friends and their parents?

3. GO...

Showing that you care and that you are interested will make your children feel good about themselves and about the friends they choose!

As a parent you can be very instrumental in expanding your child's circle of friends. Consider the following when guiding your child to accept and appreciate all children:

✔ Take your child to places where there will be a variety of children.

✔ Listen to a variety of music from all over the world.

✔ Involve your child in the community.

✔ Invite your child's friends to your home.

✔ Make an atlas a familiar book.

✔ Encourage friendships with all children.

✔ Learn how to count in another language.

✔ Go to the imported foods section of your store. Try something new.

✔ Buy books which include another language along with English.

✔ Point out the successes and achievements of all people.

✔ Find web sites which will expand your child's awareness of the diverse cultures in the world.

✔ Buy a calendar which includes celebrations from all cultures.

✔ Show that you care for all children.

✔ Adopt a foster child from another part of the world.

CELEBRATE LEARNING...

✔ Start a friendship journal—a list of your friends, special things you have done with friends, your friends' birthdays, etc.

✔ Have a friendship tea.

TO TRY LATER...

✔ Meet new friends.

✔ Compose a poem or song about friends.

✔ Do something special for a friend.

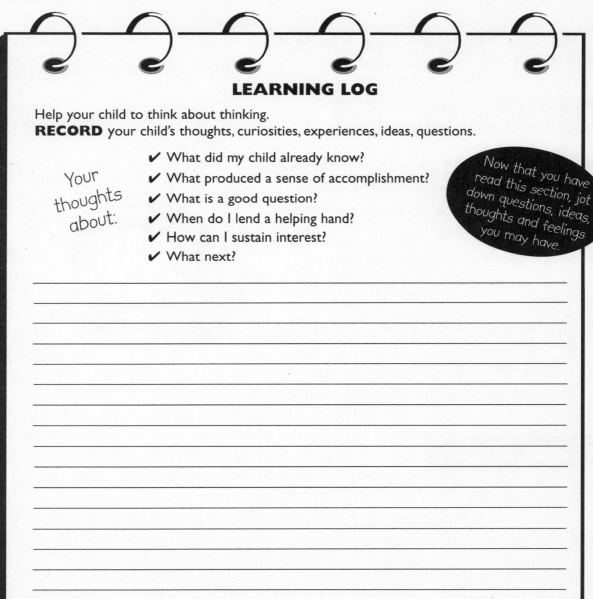

LEARNING LOG

Help your child to think about thinking.
RECORD your child's thoughts, curiosities, experiences, ideas, questions.

Your thoughts about:

✔ What did my child already know?
✔ What produced a sense of accomplishment?
✔ What is a good question?
✔ When do I lend a helping hand?
✔ How can I sustain interest?
✔ What next?

Now that you have read this section, jot down questions, ideas, thoughts and feelings you may have.

LAB #8 MEDIA MADNESS

. . . .

Watching TV, discussing advertisements, and listening to music together can be an enriching learning experience.

1. ON YOUR MARK...

Media awareness will allow you to foster the following:

✔ distinguishing between fantasy and reality

✔ recognizing and critiquing violent programs

✔ clarifying impressions

✔ discussing and creating different scenarios

✔ depicting false advertisements such as exaggerated claims

✔ increasing an understanding of commercial products.

✔ creating recording devices

✔ encouraging a sense of empowerment and control

2. GET SET...

Use the themes and stories your child likes as points for discussion.
By discussing television programs you will begin to enter your child's world and gain insightful understanding of their thoughts and feelings.

✔ How many hours a day (week) is your watching TV?

✔ Does your child see violence as an accepted way of resolving conflict?

✔ Is your child sensitive to the pain and suffering of others?

✔ Are the toys you purchase, fostering your beliefs and values?

✔ Are the lessons they learn good ones?

✔ Are scenes depicting violence emerging in your child's play?

Children enjoy make-believe and are fascinated by the stories they encounter on television, at the movies and on the Internet. Often it is difficult for children to differentiate the fictional parts of a program and the reality of what they can expect in their own world. By recreating the scenes they encounter in stories, they are learning to making sense of their world.

3. GO...

SHOWER YOUR CHILD WITH POWER!

Rather than ignoring or stopping unacceptable play that children are mimicking show children how they can recreate or change a storyline.

When children discover they have the power to change what they have witnessed an whole new and exciting world opens to them. This wondrous sense of power fuels their imagination and gives them control over their fears and anxieties. Encourage dramatizations of their stories as a way to understand, talk about and work through their fears and uncertainties.

Discuss your child's favourite programs even if they are the very ones you are wishing your child wasn't watching. Find gentle ways to make your thoughts and your child's thoughts visible.

CREATING NEW STORIES

 Dramatization

✔ Provide props to role play a story. Think of different endings the story might have.

✔ Encourage your child to think of several ways to resolve the problem in the story.

 Games

Play games about cause and effect relationships.

> I dropped a banana peel and then...
> I found a magic pen and...

Sometimes your child will see images on TV or video which depict violence. Talk openly about what she sees and how she feels about it. You can influence your child's view of the outside by taking the opportunity to discuss the difference between fantasy and reality.

Illustrations

- ✔ Illustrating the sequence of the story on separate pieces of paper.
- ✔ Mix up the original drawings and tell a new story.
- ✔ Draw different endings. Discuss your favourite ending and your child's favourite ending. Sort your endings into two piles— violent versus peaceful endings. Discuss which endings give a hopeful glimpse into what we would like our world to be.

Creating Supertoys

Take a trip to a toy store.

Design a chart to record the most popular games and toys.

i.e. Toy Store
Favourite #1
Age:
Cost:
Comments:

or—cut pictures from magazines and sort into piles based on values and beliefs.

- ✔ Discuss your child's favourite toy.
- ✔ List ideas about creating a new toy.
- ✔ Encourage and support creativity. Draw it. Make it. Use it in a variety of ways.
- ✔ The design of the product will influence the type of play that will occur.
- ✔ What materials will facilitate this?

CELEBRATE LEARNING...

✔ Find time to watch a video that both you would enjoy such as *ET* or *Black Beauty*. Discuss your favourite parts.

✔ At your next party, use magic and wonder as the theme using special effects to change a familiar story line to good from evil.

✔ Send the drawings of your new story to someone who would appreciate them. Invite them to write some text for the story.

✔ Display and show the new toy you created. Photograph the invention, frame it and hang the picture in a prominent place.

TO TRY LATER...

✔ Design a schedule of television viewing. Limit the time to one or two hours a day.

✔ Watch television together.

✔ Discuss commercials with your child. Can you find exaggerations?

✔ Call or write TV stations to express your opinion.

LEARNING LOG

Help your child to think about thinking.
RECORD your child's thoughts, curiosities, experiences, ideas, questions.

Your thoughts about:

✔ What did my child already know?
✔ What produced a sense of accomplishment?
✔ What is a good question?
✔ When do I lend a helping hand?
✔ How can I sustain interest?
✔ What next?

Now that you have read this section, jot down questions, ideas, thoughts and feelings you may have.

LAB #9 A GALLERY OF GAMES

Play games because:

- ✔ play is natural
- ✔ play is essential for children
- ✔ play is creative and spontaneous
- ✔ play is magical and complex

Games are what children love best. Games contribute to the total development of the child. You can help your child learn through the magic of games.

- ✔ play is rewarding and stimulating
- ✔ play is non-threatening
- ✔ play is non-judgmental
- ✔ play is directed by the children
- ✔ play is full of choices and decision making
- ✔ play is posing questions and hypothesizing
- ✔ play is fun, exciting, adventurous, open ended

1. ON YOUR MARK...

Playing games is a fun and exciting learning experience that will foster the following:

- ✔ using geometry and measurement
- ✔ using logic to solve problems
- ✔ posing questions
- ✔ making predictions
- ✔ creating, inventing, comparing

- ✔ getting along with others
- ✔ accepting rules
- ✔ learning and valuing games from around the world
- ✔ developing and enhancing motor skills
- ✔ extending communication skills

2. GET SET...

WHICH GAMES DOES YOUR CHILD LIKE BEST?			
card games	trivia games	memory games	matching games
board games	marble games	dice games	musical games
rhyming games	travelling games	outdoor games	indoor games

Are there games that were your favourites?

✔ Did you ever shoot marbles into holes cut into an upside down shoe box?

✔ Did you ever ask someone to guess what rhyme you were humming?

✔ Did you ever play I packed my grandmother's bag?

✔ Did you ever make up your own rules to a game and have everyone agree that these would be the rules?

3. GO...

Play all kinds of games with your child

Material for games: marble, ball, small equipment, sidewalk chalk, board, movers such as buttons, dice

Point out things that you notice

✔ Good guess

✔ You really thought about that

✔ Tell me how it works

✔ Show me how

Ask friendly questions

✔ Why did you decide to do that?

✔ Do you agree?

✔ What do you think?

✔ How did you work it out?

Create a Board Game

Start with a simple format for your game such as one that is based on moving your marker around a path. Bristol board makes a good base and index cards can be cut into quarters to use as game cards. (i.e. start—move 3 spaces, lose a turn, draw a card)

Design a Mystery Game Board

Games can be based on your child's favourite stories. Mystery stories are fun and easy to translate into board games. By using familiar stories, you are building on their interest and knowledge base. A well known favourite story is an exciting place to start. By adding new twists to the plot and creating different scenarios, you are demonstrating the art of the entrepreneur.

The best part of making games is playing it with your child.

Make Your Own Puzzles

Cut pictures from old magazines and glue onto lightweight cardboard, such as cereal boxes. Cover the picture with clear mac-tac to make it durable. Decide how large or small the puzzle pieces should be. Draw your design on the back of the picture and cut it out. Store the puzzle in an envelope.

Waiting Games

Make up a game while waiting at the dentist's office or riding on a bus. Count the number of people wearing ties, wearing something red, carrying a backpack, etc. Once you child understands the game he can create new criteria or questions.

Predict what will happen next. "How many people will be on the bus two stops later?" As you discover questions that require more advanced reasoning, find ways to record your predictions. A small notepad and pencil are useful items to have on hand.

LEARNING AT HOME WITH LEARNING LABS

Seek and Find Games

Make a list of things to find in an old newspaper or magazine i.e. A schedule, the word "found", a weather symbol, a number less than 899, the name of a province, interesting advertising, a sports score, a graph, the number 0.

Cut out the found item and display in an interesting way.

License Plate Games

Find the numbers from 1 to 25 in order. Only one number per car. Find the letters of the alphabet in alphabetical order. Add the numbers on each license plate.
Try decoding personalized plates.
Create your own codes.

4U2C

GAMES FOSTER SELF-CONFIDENCE AND EXTEND KNOWLEDGE

✔ Does your child have successful experiences?

✔ Does your child talk about her learning?

✔ Does your child see more than one way to approach a problem?

✔ Does your child apply skills to other situations?

✔ Does your child identify skills such as adding, subtracting?

GAMES FOSTER MATH TALK

Encourage the following math talk:

Attribute words: big, little, green,
Positional words: behind, under, over, in
Comparison words: bigger, taller, more, less

Ask your child how he arrived at that answer or made that decision.
Use words to describe problems we encounter in real life.
Remember that it is important to hear another point of view and
perhaps see a new way of looking at a problem.

CELEBRATE LEARNING

✔ Display puzzles, game boards etc.
✔ Invite someone to play your game.
✔ Take the game to school.
✔ Design a box for a game.

TO TRY LATER...

✔ Investigate origami and tangram puzzles.
✔ Find books about games.
✔ Learn and use sign language in a game.
✔ Tally and graph traffic patterns.

L

Think about your home and community as **LEARNING LABORATORIES. LEAD** by example by modeling your personal learning for your children. Talk about yourself as a **LEARNER. LOOK** for opportunities for family learning—visiting a library, reading aloud, exploring the outdoors.

E

EXPAND your children's thinking by involving them in new **EXPERIENCES. EXPLORE** learning opportunities throughout the home and **EXTEND** learning beyond the home. **EXAMINE** items in the outdoors...

A

ADVISE your children but do not provide all of the **ANSWERS.** Encourage them to **ANALYZE** their experiences. Ensure that you show your **APPROVAL** for their achievements and willingness to be involved in learning. Gradually help your children to move to more **ABSTRACT** thinking.

R

REVIEW knowledge and skills through interactions with your children. **REFER** to previous experiences as you explore new learning. **RELAX** and enjoy learning with your children.

N

NURTURE your children by taking care of their basic **NEEDS** for physical, emotional, and social stability. **NEGOTIATE** with your children to set relevant goals for them to reach. Involve your children in exploring **NATURE.** Accept that learning is **NOISY** and untidy.

Active Involvement

Learning is an active process that takes place in the home and throughout the community.

Learning Resources

Learning needs to be supported by a variety of materials, including recycled, commercial and natural resources.

LEARNING LABS ARE...

Learning Opportunities

Learning activities should focus on the child. Encourage discovery and free exploration. Engage in a variety of experiences.

Role of the Parent

Learning needs your participation! Celebrate success and enjoy the learning process!

LEARNING LOG

Help your child to think about thinking.
RECORD your child's thoughts, curiosities, experiences, ideas, questions.

Your thoughts about:

✔ What did my child already know?
✔ What produced a sense of accomplishment?
✔ What is a good question?
✔ When do I lend a helping hand?
✔ How can I sustain interest?
✔ What next?

Now that you have read this section, jot down questions, ideas, thoughts and feelings you may have.

LEARNING LINKS BETWEEN HOME AND SCHOOL

Part IV

By now you should be quite comfortable in understanding the concept of learning and what it looks like at home. Let's take a look at what learning looks like at school.

LEARNING IS COMMUNICATING IDEAS

Cast your mind back to your time as a learner in school. You'll probably remember learning grouped into subject areas such as language, mathematics, science, etc.

In school today you will still find these subject areas identified.

In addition to these traditional areas, schools are also concerned with promoting learning as a process which is:

interactive

purposeful

natural

on-going

personal

To do that schools provide the following:

✔ a warm, challenging environment
✔ high expectations that all children will learn
✔ opportunities to jump into real learning in many different ways
✔ explore learning resources such as books, videos, computers etc.

LEARNING LANGUAGE

One of the strongest **links** between the home and school is seen in the amazing amount of **language learning** that takes place at home before your child enters school. You provide the background experiences necessary for the school to continue to develop reading and writing skills. These background experiences begin with learning how to talk.

Right from the beginning, you naturally speak to your child and involve him in making sounds and noises as a first step in **learning language**. You help him to learn sounds, words, and sentences by telling stories, singing songs and reciting poems. This is the **rich language environment** that your child learns in at home.

One of the best things that you can do to support learning at home is to involve your child in storytelling. When children are telling stories they are expanding their ability to communicate.

THE POWER OF STORY

STORIES are a superb way to help make those connections. What stories have been passed on through your family?

How did you learn the things that you consider valuable?

How are stories shared in your family?

"When I was young..."

You made connections to things that are meaningful.

Sometimes stories are:
- ✔ written in family books
- ✔ shared using photo albums
- ✔ told at family reunions

Learning to tell stories fosters:

- ✔ creativity
- ✔ organization
- ✔ communication for meaning
- ✔ problem solving
- ✔ healthy attitudes towards learning

> Stories have natural connections for a child's learning.
> Stories engage a child in making *sense* of her world.
> They help children separate fantasy from reality.

QUESTIONS TO ASK...

- ✔ Is this story real?
- ✔ Have you heard a story like this before?
- ✔ What do you think will happen next?
- ✔ What new thing(s) did you learn in this story?

You are never too old to tell a story.
Some say that stories improve with age.

STORYTELLING = BETTER READING AND WRITING

Children who hear and tell stories move ahead faster in reading and writing. Research tells us that if a child cannot tell a story by age five, then she will not have the ability to read and understand stories at age eight.

Through listening and telling stories, children learn that stories have similar components such as:

- ✔ a setting
- ✔ characters
- ✔ a plot
- ✔ events

Your child uses this information in learning to read and write.

Discover your child's favourite stories and talk about what you like about them:

- ✔ stirring visions
- ✔ funny rhymes
- ✔ frightful episodes

- ✔ favourite characters
- ✔ magnificent illustrations
- ✔ outrageous tales

HOW CAN YOU INVOLVE YOUR CHILDREN IN STORYTELLING?

Tell your favourite stories, songs or poems aloud.
Give a child something to talk about:

> a trip to . . .
>
> we made . . .
>
> things that don't work . . .
>
> I woke up and . . .

Use wordless books or begin a story and have your child
finish it. Provide sentence starters such as "On a dark,
dark night . . ." Change the genre: mystery, science fiction,
historical. Set the mood: tell stories by candlelight.

LEARNING READING

READING is natural to young learners. They want to learn to read just like they learned to talk.

They read to make sense of their world. For instance, as you speed the modern maze of burger
palaces and toy stores, your child will quickly learn to read logos and signs. You'll know they are
reading when you can't sneak past their favourite haunts.

Print is part of their world. Children find it on:

- ✔ street signs
- ✔ stores
- ✔ restaurants
- ✔ cereal boxes
- ✔ TV guides
- ✔ computer screens

Children see others reading print in daily life by using:

- ✔ newspapers
- ✔ letters
- ✔ calendars
- ✔ cookbooks

THE ROAD TO READING

By now, children are:

- ✔ telling stories
- ✔ looking at print
- ✔ pretending to read
- ✔ finding familiar words
- ✔ choosing a book they can read
- ✔ reading on their own

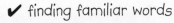

You can support reading at home by:

✔ **READING ALOUD** to your child regularly

✔ encouraging your child to read to pets, toys, siblings, friends etc.

✔ collecting a variety of reading material
such as:

- picture books
- non-fiction books
- comics
- newspapers
- computer Programs

- novels
- magazines
- flyers, ads
- instructions

✔ helping your child to choose materials she can read independently

✔ making sure that your child sees you reading regularly

READING SHOULD BE ENJOYABLE FOR EVERYONE

FAVOURITE BOOKS

MAKE FRIENDS WITH BOOKS! Make books a part of your regular family routine—borrowing books, buying books, reading books aloud, talking about books, composing books...

Become a frequent visitor to the local community and school library. Libraries can provide access to more than books. You can locate media materials such as videos and audio tapes. Libraries also offer links with community services and parent groups.

Haunt bookshops. Take advantage of opportunities that stores offer to participate in story times and author readings. Together you can enjoy the story and the sounds and rhythms of language.

Organize opportunities to share books with family and friends.

Singing songs, chanting rhymes and making silly sounds are natural and fun. Capture and extend these magic moments by finding books that continue to enchant and excite these special times.

INFANTS AND TODDLERS

CULTIVATE A LOVE FOR BOOKS!

discover treasures - read, chant & sing together
find favourite rhymes - notice illustrations - discover favourite authors

TENDER LOVING CARE

store books in a special place—bring out one or two at a time
carry in a basket or bag—repair torn pages—make book marks

RHYMES, POEMS & SONGS

Rhymes, poems & songs delight all ages, are fun and easy to memorize. Some books to look for include:

Ahlberg, Janet and Allan. *The Jolly Postman*.

Blake, Quentin. *Mister Magnolia*.

Brown, Margaret Wide. *Goodnight Moon*.

NUMBERS, COLOURS, LETTERS AND SOUNDS

Find books just have a picture and a word or two. When children begin to read along with you or when they have memorized the book and say it out loud—they are beginning to see themselves as readers.

Martin, Bill and John Archambault. *Chicka Chicka Boom Boom*.

Martin, Bill and Eric Carle. *Brown Bear, Brown Bear, What do you see?*

AGES 3 - 6 YEARS

Miles, Betty. *Hey! I'm Reading!*

Cannon, Janet. *Stellaluna*.

AGES 6 - 8 YEARS

Children of this age love to hear stories read to them, but are beginning to choose to read on their own as well. Choose from the following list of delightful tales to read to your child, and provide them with a selection of picture and chapter books for their own personal reading pleasure!

• Cole, Babette. *Princess Smartypants.*

• Feder, Paula Kurtzband. *Where Does the Teacher Live?*

• Giff, Patricia Reilly. *The Girl Who Knew It All.*

• Holmes Barbara Ware. *My Sister the Sausage Roll.*

• Lottridge, Celia Barker. *The Wind Wagon.*

• Rosner, Ruth. *I Hate My Best Friend.*

• Sadu, Itah and Roy Condy. *Christopher Changes His Name.*

AGES 8 - 13 YEARS

Children of this age have developed appreciation for particular genres that appeal to their personal tastes. They enjoy reading a series of books or titles by a favourite author. Biographies and other non-fiction material is also a popular choice for older readers.

FICTION

Children in this age group enjoy reading stories that deal with animals, mysteries, science fiction and current issues relevant to their personal world. Recommended authors include:

Babette Cole	Gordon Korman	Farley Mowat
Katherine Paterson	E. B. White	Chris Van Allsburg
Eric Wilson		

NON-FICTION

Look for books that deal with nature, science and technology as well as biographies of famous people.

Pope, Joyce. *The Children's Atlas of Natural Wonders.*

Zanella, Marianne. *The Good Housekeeping Illustrated Children's Cookbook.*

N.E. Thing Enterprises. *Magic Eye III Visions: a new dimension in art.*

Kerrod, Robin. *The Oxford Children's A to Z of Technology.*

SERIES

A number of books are published in collections or series. Look for a series that relates to your child's personal interests.

Eyewitness Books
Non-Fiction books that deal with subjects such as Medieval Life, Castles, Pyramids, Space Exploration...

I Want to Be...
Books delve into various professions

The Kingfisher Series
Offers titles such as the Young People's Book of Music and the Young's People's Book of Oceans

A home where reading is a valued part of daily life, helps your child to continue to be **SMART FROM THE START.**

A more extensive list of books is included at the back of this book.

LEARNING WRITING

Remember when you went off to make your mark on the world, and you decided to make it on the wall instead? It could be that you were expressing your earliest writing talent. Writing on the wall was not an act of mischief. You were learning to write.

When you *see the writing on the wall*, it is time to actively look for the visible signs of early writing. **WRITING,** for the young child, begins with drawing pictures and develops over time through the following stages:

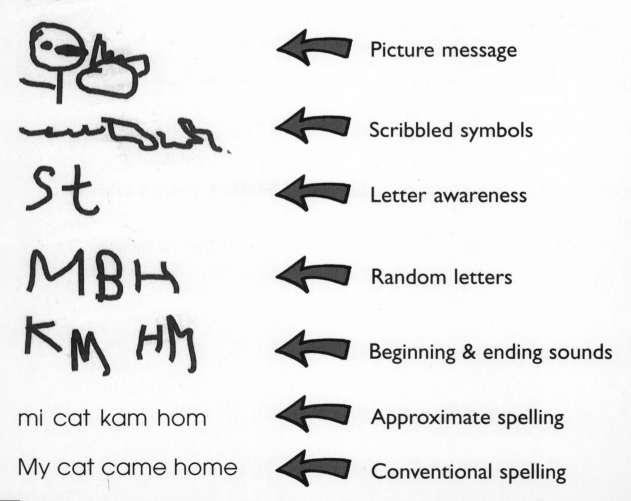

Picture message

Scribbled symbols

Letter awareness

Random letters

Beginning & ending sounds

Approximate spelling

Conventional spelling

The more experienced writer continues to draw on her experiences as a storyteller. As she writes, she learns to:

- ✔ identify a reason for the story
- ✔ thinks about who she is writing for
- ✔ moves words around to improve her story
- ✔ use correct spelling and grammar
- ✔ reads her story aloud

MOVING OFF THE WALL

It's not enough to provide a wall for writers You should also:

- ✔ find a place for your child to write
- ✔ gather materials such as:

magazines	unlined paper	crayons
lined paper	markers	pencils
erasers	chalk	stamps
cards	cardboard	string
play dough	ruler	glue
tape	hole punch	flyers
pencil sharpener	chalkboard	

- ✔ **locate a place to store writing materials**

SHARE , ENJOY, CELEBRATE WRITING

LEARNING IS MORE THAN LANGUAGE

You instinctively knew how to help your child learn to talk, read and write. But, in fact, you were doing much more than that.

You were also developing skills such as:

✔ observing

✔ classifying, sorting, ordering

✔ comparing and contrasting

✔ making generalizations

✔ gathering data

✔ asking questions

✔ communicating

✔ organizing and planning

✔ making judgements, predictions, inferences, decisions

✔ working co-operatively

✔ recording information

✔ estimating

✔ explaining

✔ designing

✔ representing

✔ recognizing relationships

✔ reflecting on learning

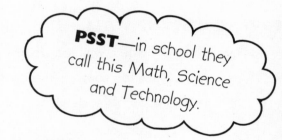

PSST—in school they call this Math, Science and Technology.

You were developing knowledge in Math, Science and Technology by:

- ✔ filling a bath tub
- ✔ sorting laundry
- ✔ collecting leaves
- ✔ keeping a growth chart
- ✔ building with blocks
- ✔ using simple machines like a can opener
- ✔ reading a map
- ✔ cooking

Working with abstract ideas

i.e. 3 = 1+2
 3 = 2+1
 3 = 1+1+1

Representing ideas in several ways
i.e. you can show three with two blocks plus
one more or with two blocks taken away
from five blocks

Connecting symbols to the real objects
i.e. three blocks is represented by the numeral 3
a three sided shape is called a triangle

Looking for patterns by classifying & sorting
i.e. the tall blocks, the heavy blocks, the red blocks, the
blocks with letters on them

Playing with 3 dimensional materials many, many times
i.e. using blocks to build towers, make roads, balance in a scale

Whew! Are you tired yet? You have been helping your child learn to talk, read, write and be a mathematician, a scientist and a technological whiz.

Guess what? You have also been helping your child to learn through the arts.

You allowed him to:

✔ explore paints, paper and material

✔ experiment with markers and crayons

✔ create sculptures from boxes and bags

✔ present puppet plays or dress up plays

✔ listen to and appreciate a variety of music

✔ learn to make musical interpretations of ideas

Learning through the **ARTS** provides your child with many important learning experiences...

✔ Children learn in other ways through their senses.

✔ Children explore, express and communicate their interests and concerns.

✔ Children watch and listen to artistic performances.

✔ Children connect with others in the community.

Our children need the arts!

Now, the moment you have been waiting for! There's just one more thing that you have taken on.

You have been helping your child to **LEARN ABOUT HERSELF AND OTHERS**. One of the ways that you have done that is by providing your child with choices such as:

making her lunch for school	**or**	making her bed
putting away laundry	**or**	sorting the socks
choosing the 7 p.m. TV program	**or**	using the computer at 7
inviting a friend to lunch	**or**	going shopping together
purchasing art supplies	**or**	subscribing to a magazine
buying new shoes	**or**	receiving an amount of money
receiving an allowance	**or**	doing some chores that earn money
making up house rules together	**or**	having parents make rules

Choices say,
"I like you
and I respect
your
decisions".

Choices

- ✔ offer options
- ✔ are a friendly but firm way of saying that this is, indeed, an expectation
- ✔ say it is time for you to be more independent and responsible
- ✔ recognize that we all have different likes and dislikes, strengths and interests

As your child begins to enter school, he will have developed a basic understanding of himself. For instance, he will understand if he prefers to learn by:

- ✔ hearing, reading or writing a story
- ✔ constructing or building
- ✔ drawing, creating maps
- ✔ listening to a CD, playing an instrument, or singing
- ✔ playing a sport, dance, swim
- ✔ learning with a friend
- ✔ learning alone

When your children begin to understand their interests, talents and learning styles, their self-esteem and confidence grows.

THEY ARE READY FOR SCHOOL!

Of course there will be other children at school.

Look at what your children can do:

- ✔ appreciate the diversity of others
- ✔ co-operate with others
- ✔ maintain relationships

You have laid important groundwork that will allow your children to learn from and with others.

As a parent, there are a number of things that you can continue to do to help your child learn about others.

Consider:

- ✔ buying a variety of books from different cultures and different parts of the world
- ✔ pointing out to your child the contributions of others
- ✔ becoming familiar with the customs and celebrations of different cultures
- ✔ answering questions your child asks about different individuals - ensure that you are being sensitive and caring
- ✔ talking about the abilities of individuals who are disabled
- ✔ discussing how television and newspapers portray individuals and groups of people
- ✔ helping your child to become a good listener and critical thinker

Knowing about others will allow your child to respect and appreciate everyone's contribution.

L

LANGUAGE LEARNING provides an strong **LINKS** between home and school. **LANGUAGE** enables the learner to make connections between previous learning and new understandings. **LEAD** your children to **LEARN** through the **LANGUAGE** of storytelling, reading and writing, mathematics, science, technology and the arts.

E

The learning **ENVIRONMENT** at home and at school is warm and challenging. High **EXPECTATIONS** are held that all children can learn. Schools and homes can provide opportunities for children to **ENGAGE** in meaningful and relevant learning.

A

Many **APPROACHES** to learning should be provided since children learn in a variety of ways. **ACCESS** to a variety of learning resources should be provided for learners at home and at school.

R

RESPECT the role of language in your children's education, and work to reinforce language. **RESPOND** to your children's questions, **RELATE** to their learning, **RECOGNIZE** their progress and **REWARD** their achievements, at home and at school. In the process you'll **REINFORCE** your children's learning.

N

NOTE the connections between home and school learning. **LEARNING** is natural, but it is **NECESSARY** to **NEGOTIATE** and **NUTURE** your children's interests and efforts.

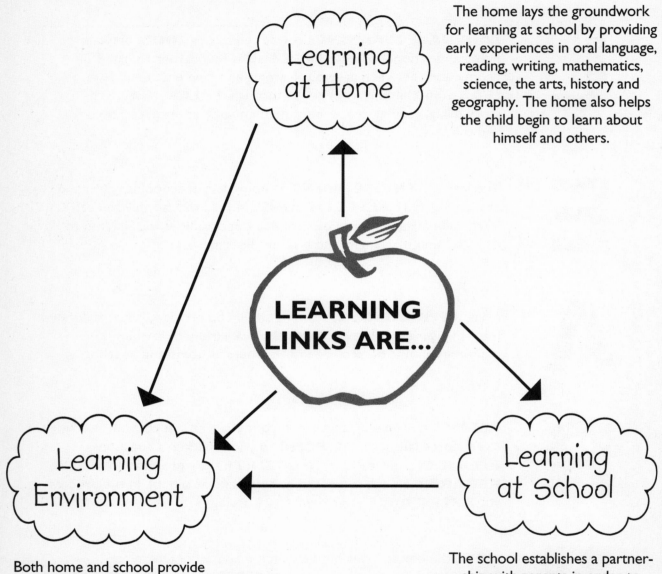

Learning at Home

The home lays the groundwork for learning at school by providing early experiences in oral language, reading, writing, mathematics, science, the arts, history and geography. The home also helps the child begin to learn about himself and others.

LEARNING LINKS ARE...

Learning Environment

Learning at School

Both home and school provide a supportive and challenging environment that meets the needs of individual learners.

The school establishes a partnership with parents in order to continue to build on active learning that progresses through a basic learning cycle.

LEARNING LOG

Help your child to think about thinking.
RECORD your child's thoughts, curiosities, experiences, ideas, questions.

Your thoughts about:

✔ What did my child already know?
✔ What produced a sense of accomplishment?
✔ What is a good question?
✔ When do I lend a helping hand?
✔ How can I sustain interest?
✔ What next?

Now that you have read this section, jot down questions, ideas, thoughts and feelings you may have.

LEARNING AT SCHOOL

Part V

HATS, HATS, HATS

As a parent it is obvious that you have taken on many roles. You have a variety of hats to wear as you continue to guide and raise your child. As far as **LEARNING** is concerned, the hats are labelled:

Learner

Learning
Theorist

Teacher

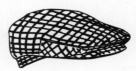

There is one more hat that can be added to your parental wardrobe. Throughout your interactions with your child, you have been gathering details about **how** she learns. You may have also collected examples of things like drawings, paintings, stories, and objects she has made from clay. As you have watched her play and explore, you have become very familiar with her preferred style of learning. You have become the **EXPERT** about your child.

Expert

Not sure that you qualify to wear this hat?

Well, let's try another pop-quiz.

Now don't panic—we don't mean to put you under fire!

This quiz will be a snap for an **EXPERT** like you.

POP QUIZ

How would you best describe your child?

✔ likes to sit and think

✔ has a large group of friends

✔ always humming

✔ requires encouragement

✔ takes risks

✔ always reading

✔ spends a lot of time on a task

✔ thinks better when walking

✔ solves problems by drawing pictures

✔ blocks out noise when working

✔ joins clubs

✔ works silently

✔ spends many hours working on a special interest

✔ needs to be busy

✔ has one special friend

✔ very quiet

✔ self-directed

✔ always asking for help

✔ always on the computer

✔ has many projects on the go

✔ thinks better when talking

✔ solves problems mentally

✔ works with a radio or TV playing

✔ prefers to work and play alone

✔ talks as he works

✔ shows concern for others

Congratulations! When it comes to your child, you are the **EXPERT**. Since you did so well on the pop quiz, you have earned your **EXPERT** credentials.

CHILD EXPERT

Presented to

_____
Insert your name

For Expert Knowledge of

_____
Insert your child's name

You have earned the privilege of wearing the **EXPERT** hat!
Now, what can you do with this new hat?
Wear it proudly to school!

SHARING YOUR EXPERTISE

Since you are the expert about your child, you have valuable information to share with the school. Your insider's point of view about him will help the school to design an appropriate learning program.

You can help the school gain insight about your child by providing information about:

✔ how he likes to learn

✔ his interests and hobbies

✔ special needs and talents he may have

✔ previous learning experiences

How to Share your Expertise

You can take advantage of a variety of opportunities to share your expertise with the school. The following are some possibilities...

✔ Participate in orientation sessions held as a child enters a new school.

✔ Participate in introductory interviews held with your child's teacher in the first school term.

✔ Arrange an opportunity to meet with your child's teacher or other school staff to discuss goals for your child.

✔ Arrange a time to share examples of work done by your child (art, writing, research etc.).

REMEMBER

School personnel have many commitments each day, just as you do. Please take time to call the school to arrange specific times for meetings with staff.

Just as you have many hats to wear as a parent, the school also puts on many hats in its job of educating your child. In fact, as you consider the learning hats that you wear, you'll see many similarities in the hats worn by the school. We have just looked at your **EXPERT HAT**. How does that hat translate when it is worn by the school?

The school wants to become an expert about each child in its care. To do that, personnel need to gather information that will tell them:

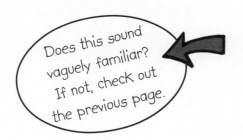

Does this sound vaguely familiar? If not, check out the previous page.

✔ how each child likes to learn

✔ the interests of each child

✔ the special needs and talents of each child

✔ the previous learning experiences of each child

To help gain this expertise the school will:

✔ talk with parents.

✔ interview the child one-on-one or through questionnaires and surveys.

✔ diagnose needs and talents through standardized testing.

✔ invite other specialized personnel such educational psychologists, speech pathologists, case workers and public health nurses to share information about the child .

✔ Should any concerns arise, please note that information from outside sources can't be gathered or shared without your permission.

So, the school goes about becoming an EXPERT about your child.

Part V — **LEARNING AT SCHOOL**

What about your other hats?
How do they compare to the role of the school?
Let's take a look...

What are your myths?

Learning is...
Learning is...
Learning is...

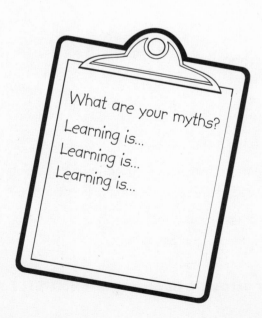

148

Through your experiences as a learner, you should be able to recognize a number of myths that are often perpetuated about **LEARNING**. Try these on for size:

Learning is not something that is done TO a learner. YOU are ACTIVELY INVOLVED in the challenging process of learning.

Since learning is very much a WORK IN PROGRESS, it is vibrant and exciting. Learning is constantly changing and adapting to the needs and style of each learner.

Learning is different things to different learners. It can't be found in a one-size-fits-all package.

Your learning experiences will have shown you that learning happens in many venues and it never stops.

LOOKING AT LEARNING IN SCHOOL

Schools also work to dispel the common myths described above. A school's approach to learning is built on the following truths...

- ✔ Schools value **LEARNING**.

- ✔ The focus of learning in the school is each individual child.

- ✔ All students are capable of learning.

- ✔ The school's programs are based on knowledge of what is developmentally appropriate for the age-stage of the children.

- ✔ Schools recognize that they must use a variety of methods to engage each child in relevant learning.

COOKING UP LEARNING

As we begin to analyze and think about how we learn and what helps us to learn, we are slipping on the hat of the **LEARNING THEORIST**.

In **Part I**, we compared learning to making a balanced meal. The main ingredients for successful learning included:

✔ a supportive environment

✔ other people

✔ high expectations

✔ opportunities to take ownership and responsibility

✔ opportunities to approximate the real thing

✔ real, relevant tasks

✔ immediate feedback

✔ opportunities to learn in a variety of ways

The school tosses these same ingredients together to make a healthy **LEARNING** meal for today's students.

Let's examine each ingredient as it appears in the school.

 Supportive Environment

The school works to create a warm environment in which each learner is valued for his unique contributions to the school community. Like a kind and judicious parent, the school pushes each learner to extend the boundaries of his knowledge and skills in order to progress. However, schools know that children will not take risks without a feeling of support from people they trust.

People

Schools know that learning occurs through interactions with others. School offers your child opportunities to learn with and from a variety of other people including classmates and staff.

High Expectations

Just as you expected your child to learn to walk and talk, schools expect all students to be able to learn. Learners will learn in different ways and at different speeds but everyone should be successful.

Opportunities to Take Ownership and Responsibility

Your child is encouraged to take **ownership** of learning at school. She gains ownership of her learning by being involved in making choices and decisions, just like you encouraged her to do at home. Your child may participate actively in:

✔ developing routines and rules for behaviour together with the teacher
  Where can we store writing material? How will we line up for recess?

✔ participating in program planning with her teacher and classmates
  What do we already know about the moon? What else should we know about the moon?

✔ **selecting learning resources**

Which *book* will I read? What *software* program will provide me with the information I need?

✔ **organizing portions of her time for learning**

My project is due in two weeks—how much will I need to do each day to meet the deadline? When should I visit the library today?

Opportunities to Approximate the Real Thing

You saw your child gradually move from babbling to speaking in complete sentences. Learning at school takes the same route. For instance, children begin with manipulating objects to develop a sense of number—what FIVE is. Then they learn to associate FIVE with the numeral 5 and later can calculate simple problems using the number 5. Gradually their learning moves from very simple concepts (five-ness) to more complex, abstract concepts (algebra). First attempts are encouraged and information is provided at the appropriate time to lead them to make connections with the next concept.

Real, Relevant Tasks

Learners learn best when they have a reason for learning. Tasks that are seen as trite or irrelevant by the learner don't "connect". As much as possible, the schools reinforce the connection between tasks and real-life applications. So, in a school's writing program, you will see students publishing their own picture books and composing a school newspaper to distribute to their peers.

Immediate Feedback

Learners need to have a sense of how they are progressing. You provide your child with feedback at home and he receives similar feedback at school. Schools praise children's efforts through words of encouragement, both orally and in written form. As much as possible, schools try to help students see learning itself as an intrinsic reward. There is nothing as satisfying as successfully completing a challenging task.

Opportunities to Learn in a Variety of Ways

Schools provide opportunities to learn in small and large groups. Children also have a chance to practice skills independently, and conduct research into areas of personal interest. Learning is supported by a wide variety of resources.

And so it is that the school is cooking up the same recipe for learning that you have been following at home.

Now, what about the role of a teacher?

TEACHER TALK

When you wear your teacher's hat, you become someone who helps to direct, instruct and coach your child's learning. When your child enters school, the teacher's role is picked by staff there.

The teacher's role in a school involves 4 key components:

✔ establishing rapport

✔ planning

✔ maintaining balance

✔ communicating

These components match what you do as you don your teacher's hat. Let's examine each component more closely to see those connections and just what happens at school.

You established a quick connection with your child directly after she was born. A teacher at school also needs to establish a bond with the children in his care. This involves gathering information about each child. Sources of information can include:

Establishing Rapport

✔ conversations with each child

✔ interviews with parents

✔ conversations with other school staff

✔ informal interest questionnaires or surveys

✔ browsing through school records

Developing rapport with students also involves establishing routines and expectations for behaviour. Doesn't this remind you of your work as a parent?

Once the teacher has some basic information about each child, he is ready to move on to the next critical component.

Planning

As a teacher, you have come to realize that learning can require planning—locating a suitable place for learning, managing a suitable time for learning, identifying your child's readiness for certain activities, gathering resources ahead of time, and assessing your child's progress. At school, where teachers are interacting with a number of children, **PLANNING** becomes even more critical. In her planning, the school teacher considers the same elements that you have been wrestling with. Planning at schools involves considering the following...

 Location - Teachers plan for learning by designing classroom space that allows for individual, small group and large group activities. In addition the teacher plans to move learning beyond the classroom to other locations—both within the school to specialized rooms such as music rooms, gyms and labs and beyond the school to places within the community such as museums and galleries.

 Time - Schools organize their days through a timetable that allows for sharing of school facilities like the gym. The teacher then organizes her class timetable to include large blocks of time devoted to various subject areas such as language, mathematics, science, the arts and history.

 Identifying Readiness - At school, teachers can rely on documents which contain descriptions of programs at each grade level. These documents have been developed to reflect what is generally expected of children at certain age or grade levels. The teacher uses this material together with her knowledge of the individuals in her class to plan an appropriate learning program. Often the teacher co-plans with other staff who are working with children at the same grade level.   In addition, students will contribute to the planning by telling what they already know about a topic and raising new questions.

 Gathering Resources - At school the teacher is responsible for purchasing resources that will support the topics of study that she will be developing at her grade level. Sometimes these resources may be stored in her personal classroom or in common storage areas which all teachers share. In addition the school provides resources through its school library. Teachers also encourage students to contribute resources to support their learning.

Assessing Progress - You noted your child's progress by observing his work and play, by gathering examples that you kept in albums and by jotting down milestones on a calendar or in a journal. Teachers at school use the same techniques. Observation plays an important role in helping a school teacher gather information about your child's progress. The teacher records her observations in record books. She will also plan tasks such as tests and demonstrations to allow students to show their skills and knowledge. Samples of students' work are gathered in files to make a record of progress over the school year. The information from all of these sources is then evaluated against the standards for the grade. For instance, students in grade 3 have their work measured against the standards for that grade. This measurement is then shared with the students and parents via report cards and interviews.

Planning is essential in helping you manage your busy days and in finding ways and time to help your child learn. At school planning continues to be a crucial part of ensuring successful learning.

A classroom teacher must maintain a balance in the pace of learning. A teacher needs to balance the types of instruction that he provides. Students receive direct instruction from the teacher as individuals and in small and large groups. They will also discuss ideas, manipulate materials and conduct research. All of these factors need to be balanced in the classroom. In your role as a teacher at home, you have come to recognize the need to balance your time, energy and resources. Balance is equally important for a teacher at school.

You learned to value time spent listening to and talking with your child. In school communication is basic to successful learning. Communication is fostered through:

Communicating

✔ conversations with students, parents and other school staff

✔ regular contact through phone call and notes

✔ written reports that are shared with students and parents

Communication with the school can be initiated by you or by the school. Maintaining open lines of communication has a direct pay-off in improving your child's learning.

HIP, HIP HURRAH

Cheerleader

This last hat reads CHEERLEADER.

You are familiar with this role through your efforts to encourage your child and celebrate her learning. A simple statement can go a long way in recognizing your child' success.

✔ I can really *see* your growth in . . .

✔ I am amazed that you know how to . . .

✔ I didn't know you could . . .

✔ I am really proud of . . .

✔ I can *see* that you are getting better at . . .

✔ I can *see* that you tried very hard to . . .

✔ I am impressed with the way that you . . .

✔ I can *see* that you are ready to . . .

✔ You are doing a good job conducting . . .

✔ I can hardly wait until your next . . .

✔ I can *see* the example of your talent in . . .

As you see the learning that your child accomplishes at school, take a few moments to celebrate his accomplishments. Time spent celebrating will really support the success of your child.

Schools also wear the **CHEERLEADER** hat as they encourage and celebrate your child's learning. A school cheers on learning by:

✔ publishing samples of student's work or photos of students involved in activities in school newsletters

✔ distributing school newsletters to local businesses

✔ hosting special event such as musicals, science fairs, and author teas

You also wear your cheerleader hat to support the work of the school. There are many ways in which you can provide support for school learning at home. Try these!

✔ Pay attention to what is happening at school.

✔ Encourage your child to make decisions that reflect a balance between school and personal needs.

✔ Support the school program by volunteering to assist in school programs and on excursions.

✔ Address parallel themes at home.

✔ Lend learning resources to the school.

✔ Monitor your child's goal setting.

✔ Establish a regular time to talk about school and learning.

✔ Model learning at home.

✔ Participate in parent-teacher interviews.

✔ Attend special school events such concerts, book fairs, guests speakers.

✔ Serve on parent-teacher committees.

✔ Share your interests and skills with students in class.

✔ Raise questions and clarifying concerns with school staff.

> You should aim to be an active partner in your child's learning. Parents and teachers need to work together to help children achieve success.

FREQUENTLY ASKED QUESTIONS

And now for some nitty, gritty. We know you have some serious questions. Here are serious answers. So sit back, pour yourself a learning cocktail from the Learning Laboratory and read on...

1. **Is my child safe at school?**

    We want all children to feel safe to learn. So students need to learn school behaviour expectations, exercise self control and to take responsibilities for the safety of self and others. Just as you do at home, the teachers in the school talk about their expectations of students and what the consequences will be. All students participate in talk about school behaviour, and their suggestions, involvement in decision making and evaluation of behaviour helps all children to be responsible for their behaviour, and as a result, to behave appropriately. Through safe school policies and practices your child will be safe at school.

2. **How will my child be disciplined at school?**

    We all know that kids can't be good all of the time. They just aren't made that way. Sometimes they slip, and this is how we can catch them at school, before they hit the ground!

    Schools catch and support "slipping" students by dealing with the child away from other curious children. Teachers will often take a student aside, or talk to her in the hall if there are concerns about behaviour. Generally speaking, most "safety nets" are made up of time out for thinking about actions, completing contacts or action plans to think through what was wrong and what they will do next time. Firm and consistent expectations are the threads that weave the safety net. Sometimes the students need still more support, at which time the school may remove student privileges, have the child call home to talk about behaviour or participate in a behaviour management program by monitoring concerns such as absenteeism, incomplete homework, rudeness or physical aggression on a daily basis. Discipline at school is not punishment. Schools, like parents, help students to learn by being calm, clear consistent and caring. After all, school must be a safe and enjoyable place for **all** children to learn.

3. **How can I get my child ready for school?**

First become informed about the school/class that your child will be entering. Talk with other families about the school and/or contact the school to talk with someone there or to arrange a visit to the site. Arrange an opportunity for you to visit the school with your child - to tour the grounds and building and to meet staff if possible. Many schools offer opportunities for students entering school for the first time or for students moving to a new division such as junior high to have orientation visits to the school. Schools also often produce information pamphlets about school routines, hours of class and necessary equipment. Become familiar with procedure for opening day in September and make sure that your child is sure about what to expect. Show your child the best route to school. If he will be riding the bus for the first time, introduce him to how to ride a bus. If possible introduce your child to another student who attends the school. Provide your child with details about when and where you will meet him when class is dismissed.

4. **How is my child graded?**

Just as the outcome of a sports game is judged by the number of goals and assists, children at school are graded according to criteria. Teachers watch your child as he works in the classroom, looking for patterns of behaviour that demonstrates what he knows and is able to do. The information is collected in many forms, including samples of his work and recorded observations. Instead of looking for a goal as is the case with hockey, the teacher looks at your child's learning according to set criteria that he is to achieve. The grades show how close your child has come to the general expectations for his level.

5. **What is the purpose of the report card?**

Before you file your child's report card away, you can use it to help your child learn even more! Look at your child's learning over a period of time. How has she progressed? What has she achieved? The report card outlines her strengths and weaknesses. It identifies her standing in her current grade level and will outline goals for improving her learning. After all, the report card is intended to be a record of learning.

6.   What should I look for in my child's report card?

There's good news and there's bad news. First, the good news. You should expect to hear how your child is doing in language, math, science, social studies and so on. You will hear of the efforts he has put forth and what his attitude is toward learning. Information about how he learns, his preferred learning style and habits will also be outlined. Look to see if your child is excited about learning. He should be, learning is very exciting! The good news is that there should not be any surprises. Any concerns about your child's learning should have been discussed well before the report card arrives in the mail. The other good news is that you are an expert now; expert learner, expert teacher, expert learning theorist and expert cheerleader. Read the report card with your various hats on and make connections between what is said in the report card and your own observations about your child's learning at home!

7.   How can I make the report card more meaningful?

Before you send the report card to grandparents, aunts, uncles and anyone else you can rope in, remember that the report card is not just for you. It is for you and your child. The most important person here is your child. Recognize her role as a learner, and read through the report card together. Put on your learner hat and think about how important the report card is as a record of her learning. Put on your theorist hat and look for learning in the teachers written words. Then, talk with your child about her learning. Try on your own teachers hat and look for important points to talk about. Discuss future areas for work and offer to help her with school work. Finally, put on your cheerleader's hat and together you can celebrate her achievements and successes—her **LEARNING!**

8. **What kinds of interviews might I have with staff at a school?**

Parent - teacher interviews provide an opportunity for both parties to discuss student learning. These interviews may follow a variety of formats and serve many purposes such as:

- **FACT FINDING**
  - Parents share information about their child with the teacher.
  - Interviews are usually held early in the school year.

- **GOAL SETTING**
  - Parents, teachers and often the student meet to set goals for learning.
  - These types of meetings are usually held once or twice during a school year.

- **PROGRESS UPDATE**
  - Parents and teachers and, occasionally, students, meet to share information about the student's progress. Samples of student work are often made available to demonstrate specific student achievement.
  - Meeting are usually held in conjunction with the distribution of report cards.

- **SPECIAL NEEDS**
  - Parents and teachers meet to discuss special needs of the student. It is often held in response to a parental request or to summarize assessments that may have been conducted by specialists or to address ongoing academic or behavioural concerns. This interview may sometimes involve other educational specialists.

9.   **How Do I Talk to The Teacher?**

Any concerns or questions which parents have about curriculum or programming may be addressed directly to the teacher. To ensure that the teacher will be available and prepared for the meeting, making an appointment by letter or by phone. If a teacher knows that a parent would like to meet, he will prepare your child's file and most recent work. As the teacher should be prepared to meet with you, ensure that you are prepared to meet with the teacher. This means that you may come prepared with a list of questions and concerns. This approach will allow you to present all the points that you have been considering and to make the best use of the limited time that may be available.

10.   **How do I establish communication with the Principal?**

Many of us are wary of approaching the principal of the school. Contrary to some public opinion, principals are mere mortals and they generally maintain an "open-door" policy and encourage members of the community to engage in dialogue with the school.

Here are some general **principles** to keep in mind when dealing with a *Principal...*

- Introduce yourself early in the school year.
- Ask about how you can help the school.
- Maintain a friendly rapport with the principal.
- Participate in school events.
- Ask questions.
- Clarify concerns—don't make assumptions based on rumours.
- Involve yourself in problem solving **with** the principal to address any concerns.
- Avoid confrontations—these situations only serve to inflame problems.
- Participate in opportunities to address school issues.

11.   **When do I talk to the Principal About Concerns?**

Most often, conferences between parents and teachers yield satisfactory results. At times, however, parents may have further questions or need additional clarification. . It is at this point that administration could be contacted. Or a situation may arise that requires immediate involvement of the principal—such as a custody issue or safety concerns such as a threat from another child.

Again, the same process in terms of readiness to meet should be followed. Here are some general guidelines that could help having a productive meeting with the principal...

- Clearly identify your child and which class he is in.

- State concisely why you want to meet or talk with the principal.

- Provide a brief background of your concerns and actions that you have taken thus far.

- Be prepared to provide a contact number or location in case the principal is not immediately available to talk with you.

- Prepare a list summarizing your questions or concerns so that you can present your issues logically and ensure that critical details are not overlooked.

- Be prepared to problem solve and negotiate contentious issues.

- Take notes and/or request a written summary of your conversation.

- Set a realistic time frame for follow up action by the principal.

- Follow up your talk or meeting with a note or phone call.

- Maintain frequent contact with the school.

12. **How can I keep my emotions under control during an interview dealing with a major issue?**

At times, conferences can become emotional when a parent or a teacher or an administrator feels that they are not being understood or heard. To ensure understanding, try the following...

- Prepare your concerns prior to the interview.
- Listen actively.
- Ask for clarification.
- Be aware of your emotional state.
- Invite a neutral party to participate in the meeting.
- Suggest that the interview be stopped if the tension becomes disruptive.
- Reschedule the meeting and try again when emotions have cooled.

13. **How does a school adapt to meet the specialized needs of my child?**

The instructional program will be modified to suit the needs of all students, particularly those who may have particular challenges. Modifications can include:

- varying the rate of instruction and consolidation of concepts
- varying the instructional level of learning resources
- providing attention to a variety of modes of instruction
- adjusting the types of expected products to suit students strengths and needs
- implementing a variety of assessment methods to ensure accurate evaluation

14. Why don't the children sit in rows anymore?

Most classrooms provide many opportunities for students to work in a variety of groupings, including working independently, in pairs, small groups of three to four students, and in large or whole class groups. Children need to be able to work on their own. However, it is becoming increasingly important that students learn how to work with others. Teamwork and cooperative learning are two abilities that will become increasingly in demand in the next few years. Our students are being prepared for these requirements through the increasing emphasis on cooperative group work in the classroom.

15. Are some children looked after better than others?

The classroom program is adaptable and supportive for the student. Within such a program the teacher supports student learning by reviewing concepts to ensure understanding, providing organizers and strategies for learning, being available for extra help, breaking down complex tasks or concepts into parts which can be mastered, using manipulatives, and conferencing with each student regularly. You can make sure that your child is well attended to by discussing questions and concerns with the teacher, and providing valuable information. By sharing information you can both help your child to learn.

16. How can I expect teachers to address bias in the classroom?

Bias in the classroom can be addressed in a number of ways. Teachers consider the make up of their students and greater society and from there they begin to design a curriculum. Teachers ensure that the materials they use are bias-free. This means that materials which portray stereotypes towards any group of individuals are unsuitable for the classroom. Teachers are also expected to actively use strategies which will allow children to develop the critical thinking skills they will need to question stereotypes whenever they encounter them. Therefore, children must know how to analyze bias critically when they are confronted by it. In developing their own awareness of bias, teachers learn all that they can about various groups of individuals. They will often ask parents to come into their classroom to do presentations. These presentations may be about their own experiences with bias or to talk about the uniqueness of various groups.

17. **What should I do if I suspect that my child is being discriminated against in the classroom?**

The most important thing to do is to conference with your child's teacher. Your child's teacher may not be aware of the impact her program has upon your child and would welcome any suggestions which would lead to a more inclusive curriculum. Make sure that you have all of your data prepared. That is, information about why you feel your child is being discriminated against. What did you hear, what did you see, what did you notice about the types of materials being used in the classroom? Most often, pointing out your concerns to the classroom teacher will result in the actions which will be satisfactory to everyone concerned.

18. **Should I talk to my child's teacher about our culture?**

Yes, most definitely! Teachers are very receptive to any information you may have which would help them to best address the needs of your child. The information you provide will help to depict your background as well as your child's experiences. Teachers are eager to include this in their curriculum so that they are able first of all, to give accurate information about a cultural group, and second, represent your child in the curriculum.

19. **What is the most effective number of children in a class?**

Recent studies have shown that when class size is under 22, teachers can make significant modifications to their instructional techniques. Most classes have more than 22 students and therefore, to modify instructional strategies.

Space and materials are directly affected by larger classes. Activity centres require more space as student are often exploring and discovering with "hands-on" materials.

Teachers are able to communicate more effectively with students and with parents with fewer students in the class.

20. **I don't know "new math". How can I help my child if I don't know how to do it?**

Teachers can provide you with summaries of how basic operations of addition, subtraction, multiplication and division are introduced and reinforced with the students. Often this type of information is made available at Curriculum Sessions or in class program summaries. New directions in mathematics have increased student involvement through activity-based programs. Providing opportunities for problem solving is the main focus for instruction. Students need to be involved in exploring new concepts and skills where they are constructing their own knowledge. You can help your child by providing opportunities for "hands on" experimentation and by recognizing the questions that they generate and encouraging their problem solving abilities.

21. **How do schools promote success for all students?**

Schools play a crucial role in providing opportunities for maximizing each child's level of performance. Schools can be equalizing factors when they articulate and model the belief that all children can learn. Schools promote successful learning opportunities when they have high expectations for **all students and** show that they care and value student thinking. Schools that encourage students to think, investigate, reflect, demonstrate and, ultimately, to be responsible for their own learning foster success for everyone.

22. **What's the best way to be informed about what is happening in the school?**

Continue to ask your child questions about his day. " How was school today ?" always gets the same answer. Probe gently. Do you have any homework? Tell me one thing you liked about school today? - Disliked? Were you on the computer today? What did you learn? Is your class planning any trips? Did you have any visitors in your classroom this week? What did they do?

Read the school newsletter. Keep a log of your own thoughts and questions. Participate in the school's Parents Association or Council.

23. Why are School Councils important?

School Councils provide an opportunity for collaboration between the community and the school. Community support is crucial to maintaining quality educational experiences for all students. It is through the contributions of individual parents that form and direction is given to the School Council. The School Council impacts on the running of the school. Get involved and help to make your community school a dynamic learning environment.

24. Why should I be involved in my child's education?

When parents are involved in their child's education, children show increased motivation and have healthier attitudes that directly result in better long term achievement. Studies show that there are fewer behaviour problems when parents take an active role.

25. How can I be involved in my child's schooling in a meaningful way?

Learning how we learn is an important first step in understanding learning. Select and try several activities suggested in the Learning Labs section of this book and assess learning while it is still occurring. Make notes of your findings.

Call your school to discover the amount of time scheduled for parent-teacher interviews. Prepare a list of your thoughts and questions to help focus the discussion.

Volunteer in significant ways that help children learn. Share your energy and enthusiasm by listening to a child read, telling a story, cooking with a small group of children, demonstrating a special skill or participating on a field trip.

WELL DONE!

L

LOOK for your children's learning at school. **LISTEN** to their thoughts and **LINGER** over discussions about what helps them to LEARN and how they **LEARN.**

E

Children learn **EVERY** day in **EVERY** way! They learn from life **EXPERIENCES** which provide concrete learning **EXAMPLES**. You can **EMPOWER** your children's **EFFORTS** and contributions to the schools' community of learners by **ENCOURAGING** them to make connections and meaning from the **EVENTS** of their lives.

A

Learning at school is organized in subject **AREAS** in varying **AMOUNTS** of time. Decisions are **ADAPTABLE, ACCOMMODATING** student strengths and needs. School **ADMINISTRATORS** are important **ALLIES** in learning. Working as a team, parents, teachers and administrators can support student **ACHIEVEMENT** to the **ADVANTAGE** of **ALL** learning partners.

R

RECOGNIZE your children's efforts at school. **REWARD** efforts with **REAL** words of praise and opportunities to extend learning at home. **RELATE** learning at home to learning at school and **RESPOND** to your children's **REFLECTIONS** about learning.

N

Children engage in learning **NATURALLY** with their own home and school **NEIGHBOURHOODS**. Parents and teachers **NEED** to **NOTICE** and **NURTURE** the connections between home and school learning.

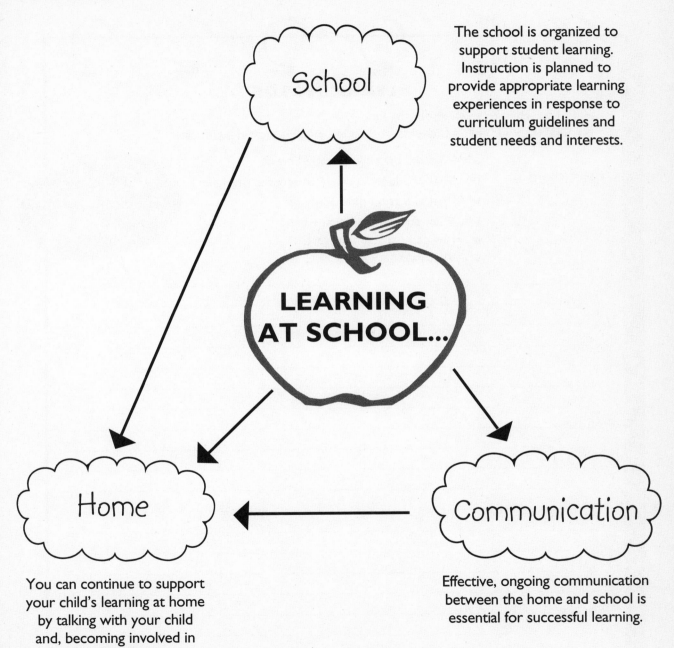

School

The school is organized to support student learning. Instruction is planned to provide appropriate learning experiences in response to curriculum guidelines and student needs and interests.

LEARNING AT SCHOOL...

Home

You can continue to support your child's learning at home by talking with your child and, becoming involved in school programs.

Communication

Effective, ongoing communication between the home and school is essential for successful learning.

LEARNING LOG

Help your child to think about thinking.
RECORD your child's thoughts, curiosities, experiences, ideas, questions.

Your thoughts about:

✔ What did my child already know?
✔ What produced a sense of accomplishment?
✔ What is a good question?
✔ When do I lend a helping hand?
✔ How can I sustain interest?
✔ What next?

Now that you have read this section, jot down questions, ideas, thoughts and feelings you may have.

LEARNING IN THE FUTURE

Part VI

THE FUTURE IMPACTS ON WHAT WE DO TODAY

Learning is the **KEY** to unlock the door to a bright future for your child. To support your child you will need to continue to take advantage of what you know from your experiences as a **LEARNER, LEARNING THEORIST**, and **TEACHER**.

PARENT AS A LEARNER

In order to cope with increased and rapid demands of the future we will all need the capacity to learn much more rapidly. You will help your child become better prepared for the future by ensuring that you:

✔ learn about learning
✔ know how you learn and how best to support your own learning

PARENT AS A LEARNING THEORIST

Continue to explore learning by:

✔ being open to change
✔ becoming informed
✔ revising your beliefs about learning as new discoveries are made
✔ re-organizing knowledge based on new research and your own life experiences

LEARNING IN THE FUTURE

Part VI

PARENT AS A TEACHER

Your role as a teacher continues as you:

✔ capitalize on learning experiences at home and in the community

✔ become responsive to the changing ways of the world

✔ model learning

✔ plan for learning

✔ celebrate successes

✔ encourage your child to become a lifelong learner

Parents and the FUTURE

The world and the demands of the work force are changing at an rapid pace. Your role as a parent is also changing. Where once you may have been acting as mainly a provider for your family, your role now includes being:

✔ a supporter and encourager

✔ a director

✔ a communicator

✔ a creative, critical thinker

✔ a listener

✔ an advisor

✔ a model of learning

✔ a collaborator

✔ an observer

✔ a questioner

✔ a problem solver

✔ a decision maker

And of course...

✔ a **LEARNING THEORIST**   ✔ a **LEARNER**   ✔ a **TEACHER**

You are now ready to add one more star to our galaxy.

And it reads **FUTURIST**

Futurist

AS A FUTURIST

Futurist

You will:

✔ polish your crystal ball

✔ respond to the changing world by thinking in new ways

✔ empower your child to learn

✔ support your child as he explores his world independently

✔ provide opportunities for your child to learn the skills required for the future

✔ provide opportunities for her to explore computer technology

TECHNOLOGY AND THE FUTURE

Parents, Children and Computers

We are comfortable in understanding helping our children develop literacy in the traditional sense of reading, writing, speaking and listening. Computer literacy is now another essential element in our children's education.

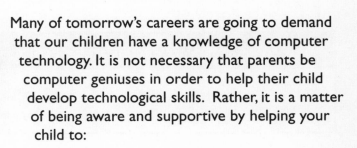

In order to prepare themselves for the future, it is essential that children have opportunities to interact with computer technology. They can discover the uses and implications of such technology thorough experiences using computers at school, at home and at community locations such as libraries.

Many of tomorrow's careers are going to demand that our children have a knowledge of computer technology. It is not necessary that parents be computer geniuses in order to help their child develop technological skills. Rather, it is a matter of being aware and supportive by helping your child to:

LEARNING IN THE FUTURE

Part VI

✔ become familiar with the application of technology in our daily tasks

using bank machines, answering machines, fax machines . . .

✔ understand how to employ computers to access information and process data

using software and CD ROM technology, using basic data bases, accessing information from the World Wide Web

✔ use computers to communicate and collaborate with others

using word processing programs to record and compose, using electronic mail, posting information on the World Wide Web

✔ use computers to support self-directed learning

accessing information from a variety of sources

You have given your children a **SMART START**. Now, lead them into a smart future by helping them to . . .

- ✔ learn effectively and efficiently
- ✔ know how to find and use the resources they need
- ✔ take responsibility for themselves, their communities and their world
- ✔ solve problems and make responsible decisions
- ✔ listen and communicate effectively
- ✔ think critically and creatively
- ✔ act logically
- ✔ demonstrate self-esteem and confidence
- ✔ plan and work effectively with others
- ✔ respect the thoughts and ideas of others
- ✔ take responsibility for collaborative problem solving and negotiation
- ✔ take on leadership roles when appropriate
- ✔ interact with others honestly and with integrity
- ✔ demonstrate initiative and persistence
- ✔ participate as responsible citizens
- ✔ set goals
- ✔ make wise and safe choices for healthy living
- ✔ maintain a positive attitude towards change
- ✔ use technology and information systems effectively

BLINDING FLASH OF INSIGHT
That is where this book comes in!

LEARNING IN THE FUTURE

L

E

A

R

N

LEARNING is the **KEY** to future success. You will need to provide **LEADERSHIP** for your children by continuing to be a **LEARNER** who is open to change.

You will **EMPOWER** your children by facilitating and supporting their personal learning. You will need to **EMBRACE** the changes that the future offers. You will help your children to develop the **EMPLOY-ABILITY** skills that future jobs will require.

You will need to continue to be **AWARE** of new developments and be **ALERT** to the latest discoveries in the world. By providing opportunities for your children to take **ADVANTAGE** of technological tools, you will promote future success for your children. The world of work in the future will demand the **ABILITY** to be **ADAPTABLE**.

Change will occur at a **RAPID** pace in the future. Our children will need to be **RESOURCEFUL** and **READY** to deal with change in a proactive way. Being able to learn independently and **REFLECT** on their learning will be crucial to future success.

Learners of the future will be **NAVIGATING** in exciting, unchartered waters. It is **NECESSARY** to be prepared to deal with the pace of the future by continuing to focus on learning.

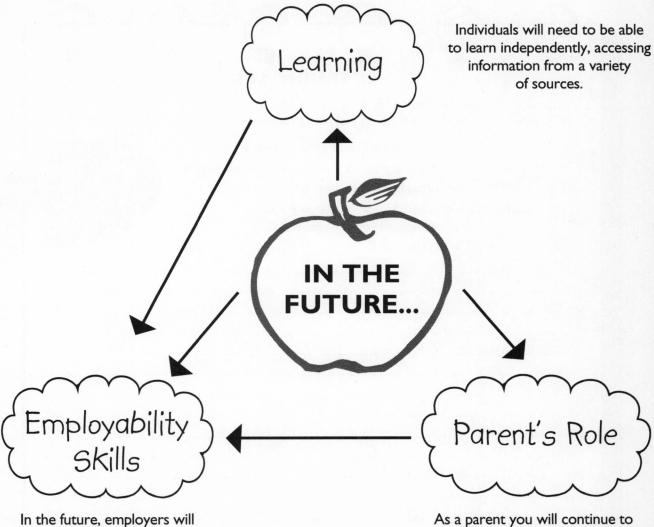

Learning

Individuals will need to be able to learn independently, accessing information from a variety of sources.

IN THE FUTURE...

Employability Skills

In the future, employers will require that individuals be able to think critically, communicate effectively, display a positive attitude toward change and demonstrate teamwork skills.

Parent's Role

As a parent you will continue to develop your skills as a learner, teacher, theorist and futurist.

LEARNING IN THE FUTURE

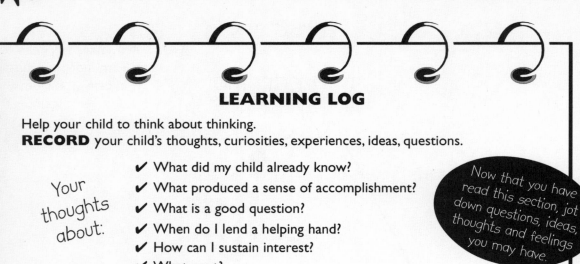

LEARNING LOG

Help your child to think about thinking.
RECORD your child's thoughts, curiosities, experiences, ideas, questions.

Your thoughts about:

✔ What did my child already know?
✔ What produced a sense of accomplishment?
✔ What is a good question?
✔ When do I lend a helping hand?
✔ How can I sustain interest?
✔ What next?

Now that you have read this section, jot down questions, ideas, thoughts and feelings you may have.

_____

_____

_____

_____

_____

_____

_____

_____

_____

_____

_____

_____

_____

_____

_____

APPENDICES

APPENDIX 1
LESSONS IN LEXICON

As you continue to explore learning, it will be helpful to have a common language about learning that you can use to communicate with others. It is so easy to become confused with the general hub-bub of edu-babble and the jargon often used in schools. You need to be comfortable with the LEXICON.

Naturally it would not be appropriate for us to simply provide you with a list of terms. Having read *Smart From the Start*, you know that learning should involve you in problem solving. You also know that learning should be playful and enjoyable. So our last lesson for you is to help guide you in developing a collection of terms for your personal learning glossary. We have identified some terms that you may encounter along with potential definitions. Your task is to use your current knowledge to consider the definitions being offered and make an informed choice!

So fire up your dendrites and have a go . . . .

The Lexicon	Choice 1		Choice 2
abstract thinking	how Picasso thought	or	collecting your thoughts to form a theory
achievement	reaching the top of Mount Everest	or	a demonstration of learning
accountability	what kids do on their fingers	or	to explain one's actions
active learning	what aerobic instructors do	or	being involved in learning
approximate spelling	coming close in a spelling bee	or	using basic phonics to begin writing
assessment	choosing the best donkey	or	gathering information about learning

authentic learning	a reality check	or	real life learning
benchmark	graffiti on a bench	or	points of reference to measure progress
celebrate	dendrites going wild	or	recognizing learning
cognitive	what your mechanic does to your car	or	thinking
collaborative	what the dry cleaner does to your shirt	or	working with others
comprehension	droplets of water jelling together	or	understanding fully
conference	a party in prison	or	a meeting to share information
constructivism	what a high steel worker does	or	constructing new knowledge from existing knowledge
consolidation	making a jell-o mold	or	connecting your learning to a new idea
curriculum	a babbling brook	or	your school's course of study
demonstrate	a marketing strategy	or	showing what you know
dialogue journal	Jack Frost's colouring instructions	or	written talk between teachers and students
engaged	sporting a sparkler	or	actively involved in learning
evaluation	the value assigned to the letter "e"	or	a judgment based on learning data

expectation	a pregnant woman	or	what the learner will achieve
grading	what a bulldozer does on the road	or	describing achievement by assigning a grade
intellect	a sign on a voting booth	or	the capacity for knowledge
intermediate	food you eat at intermission	or	usually grades 7 and 8
investigate	a fence at an investment firm	or	to examine closely
junior	a name for your child	or	grades 4 to 6
learning styles	clothes you wear to learn in	or	your natural learning preferences
monitoring	cleaning your computer screen	or	to watch with a purpose
multiple intelligences	smart twins	or	different ways of knowing
peer assessment	looking over the end of your dock	or	comment on each others work
portfolio	a seaport	or	a collection of student learning
primary	the first step of an election	or	actively involved in learning
reflection	a collection of knee jerks	or	thinking about your learning
reporting	docking over and over	or	communicating student achievement
rubrics	geometric puzzles	or	a scale for rating student learning
standards	high jump poles	or	criteria used to measure student progress

APPENDIX 2
BEAUTIFUL BOOKS

Infants and Toddlers

The following books are recommended as resources and are presented in age appropriate categories.

RHYMES, POEMS & SONGS

Rhymes, poems & songs delight all ages, are fun and easy to memorize. Some books to look for include:

- Ahlberg, Janet and Allan. *The Jolly Postman*. Toronto: Heinemann Ltd., 1986. 0434925152

- Blake, Quentin. *Mister Magnolia*. London: Harper Collins, 1980. 0006618790

- Brown, Margaret Wise. *Goodnight Moon*. New York: Harper Collins, 1997. 0060275049

- De Paola, Tomie. *Favourite Nursery Tales*. New York: Putnam's Sons, 1986. 0399213198

- Gilman, Phoebe. *The Wonderful Pigs of Julian Jiggs*. Toronto: Scholastic Canada Ltd., 1988. 0590748475

NUMBERS, COLOURS, LETTERS & SOUNDS

Find books that just have a picture and a word or two. When children begin to read along with you or when they have memorized the book and say it out loud, they are beginning to see themselves as readers.

- Carle, Eric. *The Mixed-Up Chameleon.* New York: Harper, 1984.   0690043961

- Hutchins Pat. *Good-Night, Owl.* New York: Simon and Schuster, 1972.   0689713711

- Jam, Teddy and Eric Beddows. *Night Cars.* Toronto: Groundwood/Douglas and McIntyre, 1988.   0888991347

- Martin, Bill and John Archambault. *Chicka Chicka Boom Boom.* New York: Simon and Sschuster, 1989.   067167949X

- Martin, Bill and Eric Carle. *Brown Bear, Brown Bear, What Do You See?* New York: Holt, 1983.   0805017445

- Wildsmith, Brian. *Brian Wildsmith 123.* Brookfield, CN: Millbrook Press, 1965.   1562949055

AGES 3-6 YEARS

- Briggs, Raymond. *The Snowman.* Toronto: Penguin, 1978.   0140503501

- Burningham, John. *Where's Julius?* London: Random House, 1986.   0099200716

- Cannon, Janet. *Stellaluna.* New York: Harcourt Brace, 1993.   0152802177

- Ehlert, Lois. *Feathers for Lunch.* New York: Harcourt Brace, 1990.   0152009868

- Marshall, James. *Fox Outfoxed.* Toronto: Penguin, 1992.   0140381139

- Miles, Betty. *Hey! I'm Reading!* New York: Knopf, 1995.   067995644

- Munsch, Robert. *Millicent and the Wind.* Toronto: Annick Press, 1984.   0920236936

AGES 6 to 8 YEARS

Children of this age love to hear stories read to them, but are beginning to choose to read on their own as well. Choose from the following list of delightful tales to read to your child, and provide them with a selection of picture and chapter books for their own personal reading pleasure!

- Cole, Babette. *Princess Smartypants.* London: Harper Collins, 1986.   0006627986

- Feder, Paula Kurtzband. *Where Does the Teacher Live?* Toronto: Penguin, 1979.   0140381198

- Giff, Patricia Reilly. *The Girl Who Knew It All.* New York: Bantam Doubleday Dell, 1979.   0440428556

- Holmes Barbara Ware. *My Sister the Sausage Roll.* New York: Hyperion, 1997.   078681182X

- Lottridge, Celia Barker. *The Wind Wagon.* Toronto: Douglas and McIntyre, 1995.   0888992343

- Rosner, Ruth. *I Hate My Best Friend.* New York: Hyperion, 1997.   0786811692

- Sadu, Itah and Roy Condy. *Christopher Changes His Name.* Toronto: Scholastic, n.d.   0590246240

AGES 8 TO 13 YEARS

Children of this age have developed appreciation for particular genres that appeal to their personal tastes. They enjoy reading series of books or titles by a favourite author.

NON - FICTION
Look for books that deal with nature, science and technology as well as biographies of famous people.

- Krull, Kathleen. *Lives of the Musicians: Good times bad times (and what the neighbours thought)* San Diego: Harcourt, Brace, 1996. 0152480102

- Kerrod, Robin. *The Oxford Children's A to Z of Technology.* Oxford University Press, 1996. 0199103593

- N.E. Thing Enterprises. *Magic Eye III Visions: a new dimension in art..* Kansas City: Andrews & McNeel, 1994. 0836270177

- Platt, Richard. *Stephen Biesty's Everything Incredible: How Things are Made - From Chocolates to False Teeth and Race Cars to Rockets.* Toronto: Dorling Kindersley/Scholastic Press, 1996. 0590124064

- Platt, Richard. *Stephen Biesty's Incredible Explosions.* Toronto: Dorling Kindersley/Scholastic Press, 1996. 0590248836

- Pollard, Michael. *100 Greatest Men.* Limsfield, Great Britain: Dragon's World Books, 1995. 1850283060

- Pope, Joyce. *The Children's Atlas of Natural Wonders.* Brookfield Ct.: Millbrook Press, 1995. 1562948865

- Royston, Angela. *100 Greatest Women.* Limsfield, Great Britain: Dragon's World Books, 1995. 1850283079

- Zanella, Marianne. *The Good Housekeeping Illustrated Children's Cookbook.* New York: Morrow Books, 1997. 0688133754

SERIES

A number of books are published in collections or series.

Eyewitness Books

Non-Fiction books that deal with subjects such as Medieval Life, Castles, Pyramids, Space Exploration . . .

• Ardley, Neil. *Music*. Toronto: Dorling Kindersley/Stoddart Publishing, 1989.   0773722645

• Cotterell, Arthur. *Ancient China*. Toronto: Dorling Kindersley/Stoddart Publishing, 1994.   0773728090

• Langley, Andrew. *Medieval Life*. Toronto: Dorling Kindersley/Stoddart Publishing, 1996.   0773729313

• Redmond, Ian. *Gorilla*. Toronto: Dorling Kindersley/Stoddart Publishing, 1995.   0773228783

• Stott, Carole. *Space Exploration*. Toronto: Dorling Kindersley/Stoddart Publishing, 1997.   077373029X

• Wilkinson, Phillip. *Building*. Toronto: Dorling Kindersley/Stoddart Publishing, 1995.   0773728449

I Want to Be . . .

Books delve into various professions.

- Grace, Catherine O'Neill. *I want to be an Astronaut.* San Diego: Maze Productions/Harcourt Brace & Company, 1997. 0152013008

- Grace, Catherine O'Neill. *I want to be a Dancer.* San Diego: Maze Productions/Harcourt Brace & Company, 1997. 0152012990

- Grace, Catherine O'Neill. *I Want to be an Engineer.* San Diego: Maze Productions/Harcourt Brace & Company, 1997. 0152012982

The Kingfisher Series

Offers titles such as the Young People's Book of Music and the Young People's Book of Oceans

- Wilson, Clive (ed.) *The Kingfisher Young People's Book of Music.* New York: Kingfisher Books, 1996. 24681097531

- Lambert, David. *The Kingfisher Young People's Book of Oceans.* New York: Kingfisher Books, 1997. 0753450984

- Steele, Philip. *The Kingfisher Young People's Atlas of the World.* New York: Kingfisher Books, 1997. 0753450860

APPENDIX 3
FURTHER READING

We've divided our suggested further reading into two sections. The first is a small selection of parenting resources and the second is a selection of only a few resources that form part of the background for education in the classroom. What we've hoped to provide here is merely a starting point for your own learning experience!

PART A

- Bettelheim, Bruno and Anne Freegood. *A Good Enough Parent: A Book on Child Rearing.* New York: Random House, 1987. 0394757769

- Brazelton, T. Berry. *On Becoming a Family.* New York: Delacorte/Seymour Lawrence, 1992. 0385307683

- Brazelton, T. Berry. *Touchpoints: Your Child's Emotional and Behavioural Development.* Reading, Mass: Addison-Wesley, 1992. 0201093804

- Clay, Marie. *Writing Begins at Home: Preparing Children for Writing When They Go to School.* Portsmouth, N.H.: Heinemann, 1988.

- Coloroso, Barbara. *Kids are Worth It.* Toronto, Somerville, 1995. 1895897572

- Cosby, Bill. *Fatherhood.* Garden City, New York: Doubleday, 1986. 0425097722

- DeBono, Edward. *Teaching Your Child How to Think.* London: Viking, 1992. 0670830135

- Drescher, John M. *When Your Child is 6 to 12.* Intercourse, PA: Good Books, 1993. 1561480940

- Faber, Adele and Elaine Mazlick. *How to Talk so Kids Will Listen—And Listen so Kids Will Talk.* New York: Avon, 1980. 0380570009

- Graves, Donald and Virginia Stuart. *Write from the Start: Tapping Your Child's Natural Writing Ability.* New York: New American Library, 1985.

cont'd

- Greenspan, Stanley I. *Playground Politics*. Reading, Mass: Addison-Wesley, 1993.   0201570807

- Healy, Jane M. *Your Child's Growing Mind*. Garden City, N.Y.: Doubleday, 1987.   0385231490

- Hunter, Dette and Jocelyn Shipley. *Making Your Own Traditions*. Newmarket, ON: Traditions Press, 1988.

- Lambert-Lagace, Louise. *Feeding Your Child*. Toronto: Stoddard, 1984.   0773750177

- Leach, Penelope. *Your Baby and Child from Birth to Age Five*. New York: Knopf, 1989.   0394579518

- McCutcheon, Randall. *Get Off My Brain*. Minneapolis, MN: Free Spirit Publishing, 1985. 0915793024

- Mithaug, Dennis. *Self-Determined Kids*. Lexington, Mass.: D.C. Heath, 1991.   0669271403

- Newman, Susan. *Little Things Long Remembered*. New York: Crown, 1993.   0517593025

- Nierenberg, Gerard. *The Art of Creative Thinking*. New York: Simon and Schuster, 1982. 034612559.6

- Shapiro, Stanley and Karen Skinulis. *Parent Talk*. Toronto: Harper and Stoddard, 1997.   0773758585

PART B

- Armstrong, Thomas. *Multiple Intelligences: In the Classroom*. Alexandria: Association for Supervision and Curriculum Development, 1994.   0871202301

- Booth, David and Carol Thornley-Hall. *Classroom Talk*. Portsmouth, N.H.: Heinmann, 1991.   092121765X

- Cambourne, Brian. The Whole Story: *Natural Learning and the Acquisition of Literacy in the Classroom*. New York: Ashton Scholastic, 1988.   0908643497

- Charles, Randall and Frank Lester and Phares O'Daffer. *How to Evaluate Progress in Problem Solving*, Reston, Va.: National Council of Teachers of Mathematics, 1987.   0873532414

- Davies, Anne, Caren Cameron, Colleen Politano and Kathleen Gregory. *Together is Better: Collaborative Assessment & Reporting*. Winnipeg: Peguis, 1992.   1895411548

- Edwards, Carolyn, Lella Gandini and George Forman. *The Hundred Languages of Children*. Norword, New Jersey: Ablex, 1993.   089391-9276

- Esler, William and Mary Esler. *Teaching Elementary Science*. Belmont California: Wadsworth, 1996.   0534505112

- Frazee, Bruce and Rose Ann Rudnitski. Integrated Teaching Methods. Albany, New York: Delmar, 1995.   0827359594

- Gibbs, Jeanne. *Tribes*. Santa Rosa, Ca.: Centre Source, 1994.   0932762093

- Grant, Janet Millar, Barbara Heffler and Kadri Mereweather. *Student-Led Conferences*. Markham, Ontario: Pembroke, 1995.   1551380544

- Holdaway, Don. *Independence in Reading*. Sydney: Ashton Scholastic, 1980.   0868961140

- Kagan, Spencer. *Cooperative Learning*. San Juan Capistrano, Ca: Kagan, 1992. 1879097109

- Katz, Lillian and Sylvia Chard. *Engaging Children's Minds: The Project Approach*. Norwood, N.J.: Ablex, 1992. 0893915432

- Mathematical Association (UK) *Math Talk*. Portsmouth, N.H.: Heinmann, 1987. 0435083074

- Newman, Judith. *Finding Our Own Way*. Portsmouth, N.H.: Heinmann, 1990. 0435085018

- Pollishuke, Mindy and Susan Schwartz. *Creating the Child-Centred Classroom*. Toronto, Canada: Irwin, 1990. 0772517223

- Richards, Roy. *An Early Start to Technology*. Hemel Hempstead, Great Britain: Simon & Schuster, 1991. 0750100338

- Schwartz, Susan and Maxine Bone. *Retelling, Relating, Reflecting*. Toronto: Irwin Publishing, 1995. 0772520984

- Sorenson, Juanita, Lynn Buckmaster, Mary Kay Francis and Karen Knauf. *The Power of Problem Solving*. Boston: Allyn and Bacon, 1996. 0205159435

- Strickland, Dorthy and Lesley Morrow. *Emerging Literacy: Young Children Learn to Read and Write*. Newark, DE: International Reading Association, 1989. 0872073513

- Wells, Gordon and Gen Ling Chang-Wells. *Constructing Knowledge Together: Classrooms as Centres of Inquiry and Literacy*. Portmouth, N.H.: Heinmann, 1992. 0435087312

- Wright, Ian. *Elementary Social Studies*. Scarborough: Nelson Canada, 1995. 0176042008

INDEX

CHILD EXPERT

Presented to

Insert your name

FOR EXPERT KNOWLEGE OF

Insert your child's name